Instructor's Manual and Suggested Solutions

to Accompany

The Integrated Audit Practice Case

Fourth Edition

David S. Kerr
Randal J. Elder
Alvin A. Arens

The ***Integrated Audit Practice Case*** is based on the principle that learning is best achieved through hands-on experience. Although auditing textbooks and good teachers are important in the learning process, they are not sufficient. Our experience in developing and experimenting with these materials over several years is that students significantly improve their understanding of the auditing process by completing the ***Integrated Audit Practice Case***.

Students typically have the most difficulty understanding such things as materiality and inherent risk and how they affect the rest of the audit; assessing control risk from flowcharts and internal control questionnaires and how these assessments affect tests of controls and the rest of the audit; and the relationships among analytical procedures, tests of controls, substantive tests of transactions, and tests of account balances. The ***Integrated Audit Practice Case*** is designed specifically to help students understand these relationships.

Recommendations for Use of the Integrated Audit Practice Case

We recommend that each student complete his or her own practice case independently. The use of groups to do the practice case diminishes its effectiveness as a teaching tool. However, we encourage students to compare their answers after they have completed each assignment and to make corrections as they feel appropriate.

To reduce grading time, some instructors prefer to have students work in groups and turn in just one practice case per group. In these situations, we recommend that the instructor encourage each student to first complete his or her own practice case independently, then meet as a group to discuss the practice case and to compile their group answers to be turned in for grading. Alternatively, the instructor could randomly select one student in each group to turn in his or her case for grading, with each member of the group receiving the score earned on that case. Another approach is to have one group member prepare each workpaper, and the other group members review the workpaper, with students alternating roles. This approach is particularly effective for groups of two students.

Because the case is integrated, your on-going involvement with the case for each assignment is essential. We have found that three things are helpful:

1. Spend a few minutes in class going over the requirements for each assignment, including any deletions, before students begin their work.

    Prior to Assignment 1, you should inform students whether you would like them to:

    *   complete all workpapers manually without using a computer, or

    *   use a personal computer to complete the *Excel* workpapers and print out copies for grading, or

    *   use a personal computer to complete the *Excel* workpapers, and save and submit the *Excel* workpaper file for grading.

2. Grade each assignment and return it to the students as quickly as possible to provide feedback for the next assignment.

3. Discuss each completed assignment when you return it to make sure students understand the related concepts and judgments.

Deleting / Modifying Assignments and Requirements

Since a primary objective of this case is to help students understand how the various parts of an audit "fit" together, we encourage instructors not to omit any of the assignments or alter the order in which they are assigned. However, there may be circumstances in which time constraints require flexibility in the use of the case.

At the end of each assignment, you will find several "discussion questions". These questions are included to help students better understand the concepts in each assignment. These can be deleted without affecting other parts of the case.

The following guidelines are provided for instructors who choose not to assign all 10 assignments, or who want to modify the order in which assignments are given.

Assignments 1, 2, and 3 — Audit Planning Phase:

- Assignments 1, 2, and 3 focus on the audit planning phase. Assignment 1 provides students with important background information about the client. If you choose to omit Assignment 1, be sure to have students read the client background information in the *Permanent file* prior to beginning any other assignments. Students should also be instructed to read the *Introduction to the Integrated Audit Practice Case* and to follow the workpaper preparation guidelines found in the *Introduction* when completing each assignment.

- We strongly recommend that you do not omit Assignment 2 (preliminary analytical procedures) or Assignment 3 (materiality and risk) since portions of subsequent assignments are based on decisions made in these two assignments.

Assignments 4 and 5 — Internal Control / Tests of Controls and Substantive Tests of Transactions:

- Assignment 4 involves completion of an internal control questionnaire, preliminary assessment of control risk and designing tests of controls and substantive tests of transactions. In Assignment 5, students perform tests of controls and substantive tests of transactions. We strongly recommend that you do not omit, or change the order of, either of these assignments.

Assignments 6, 7, 8, and 9 — Substantive Tests of Account Balances:

- Assignments 6 through 9 deal with the audits of accounts receivable, accounts payable, cash, and inventory. Since these four assignments are independent of one another, you can omit one or more of these assignments without affecting the remaining assignments.

- Assignment 6 (audit of accounts receivable) can be completed using non-statistical sampling (option A), monetary unit sampling (options B and C), or difference estimation (option D). You should inform your students which of these four options you would like them to use. You can also assign more than one method to allow students to compare outcomes under different sampling methods.

Assignment 10 — Complete the Audit:

Since this assignment illustrates how the various phases of an audit are tied together, helps students understand what is involved in completing an audit, and brings the case to closure, we strongly recommend that this assignment not be omitted.

Guidelines for Grading

1. To encourage students to take the project seriously, we recommend assigning the case at least 25% of the course grade.

2. When grading the assignments, we emphasize apparent effort and completion of all parts of each assignment. Because there are a number of requirements in the case requiring the use of judgment, students are not expected to produce identical solutions. As in practice, there are various supportable answers. Although we provide guidance on rounding throughout the case, students' numerical answers may vary slightly due to rounding.

3. Auditing students should be encouraged to complete each assignment neatly and professionally. We tell students that their work will be graded on the basis of (1) neatness, (2) completeness, (3) accuracy, and (4) the reasonableness of their judgments. We ask students to prepare their assignments in the manner in which they would submit similar work to a hypothetical employer. Students are expected to initial and date each workpaper they complete. Student initials are indicated by "**XX**" throughout the solutions manual.

4. Since the focus is on learning, we typically grade assignments rather quickly and leniently to facilitate quick turn-around time. We inform students that they will lose points for sloppy or incomplete work.

5. Some instructors have students exchange completed assignments and grade them in class. This approach reduces grading time for the instructor while facilitating quick turn-around time for the students. However, if you use this approach, you should be sure to give students clear grading instructions and ask students to sign their name on the paper(s) they are grading (to assign responsibility and encourage careful grading).

6. To ensure students have submitted their own work and not simply reprinted another student's solutions, check the following:
    *   Scan for the student's initials on the top right corner of each workpaper.
    *   Audit steps in the audit programs that were performed by the student should be initialed by the student.
    *   Ensure all submissions are original documents completed by the student in pencil, *not* photocopies.

For your convenience, sample grading sheets for each assignment are provided on the following pages. The grading sheets contain cross-references to the related assignment requirement and workpaper number where the work should be performed. The solutions follow in workpaper number order, and the solutions and other information to be completed by the students are indicated in bold on each workpaper. The answers to the discussion questions are located at the back of the solutions manual, behind the workpapers.

The grading sheets are based on the allocation of points shown below. (Note: the sample grading sheets do not include points for the discussion questions at the end of the assignments.)

Assignment	Topic	Points
1	Review client background information	4
2	Perform preliminary analytical procedures	10
3	Determine materiality and assess risks	8
4	Assess control risk and plan tests of controls	10
5	Perform tests of controls and transactions	10
6	Perform audit of accounts receivable	15
7	Perform audit of accounts payable	15
8	Perform audit of cash	8
9	Perform audit of inventory	10
10	Complete the audit	10
	Total points possible =	100

The grading sheets are designed to minimize the time spent grading the case. The sheets are formatted to have any deductions subtracted from the maximum possible score, and no entries are required on the grading form unless there is a deduction. Some instructors prefer to award points for the work completed, or change the point allocations for individual case requirements. Please feel free to modify the grading sheets as you believe appropriate for your classes.

Assignment 1 (4 points)

Student Name _____

Purpose of assignment

- To familiarize you with the client's background and industry information.
- To ensure you know what should be included in engagement letters.

Points allocation

			Your Points	Possible Deductions
		Total points possible (maximum point loss possible)	**4**	**–4**
Reqrmt.[1]	W/P			
1.b.	**4-1**	Missing reference to GAAP in engagement letter	–_____	–2
1.b	**4-1**	Missing reference to GAAS in engagement letter	–_____	–2
		Total points earned	_____	

---

[1] Refers to the Audit Performance Requirements in the assignment.

Assignment 2 (10 points)

Student Name _____

Purpose of assignment

- To ensure you are familiar with the purposes of preliminary analytical procedures.
- To ensure you know how to perform preliminary analytical procedures.

Points allocation

			Your Points	Possible Deductions
		Total points possible (maximum point loss possible)	**10**	**−10**
Reqrmt.	**W/P**			
2.b.	**2-1**	Missing or inaccurate calculations of profitability / performance ratios	− _____	−1
2.c.	**2-2**	Missing or inaccurate commentary on trends in profitability ratios	− _____	−1
2.d.	**2-3**	Missing or unreasonable assessment of financial condition	− _____	−1
2.e., 2.f.	**2-4-a, 2-4-b**	Missing, incomplete, or unreasonable identification of fluctuations and significance	− _____	−1 to −2
2.g.	**2-5-a, 2-5-b**	Missing, incomplete, or unreasonable analysis of income statement fluctuations	− _____	−1 to −2
2.h.	**93-1, 93-2**	Missing additions to management letter	− _____	−1 to −2
	2-1 to 2-5-b, 93-1	Missing student's initials or date in top right corner of workpapers completed by student.	− _____	−1
		Total points earned	_____	

Assignment 3 (8 points)

Student Name _____

Purpose of assignment

- To ensure you are familiar with how materiality and risk levels are determined in an audit.

Points allocation

			Your Points	Possible Deductions
		Total points possible (maximum point loss possible)	**8**	**–8**

Reqrmt.	W/P		Your Points	Possible Deductions
3.b.	**5-1**	Missing or unreasonable inherent risk assessments	–_____	–1
3.c.	**5-2-a, 5-2-b**	Missing or unreasonable assessment and justification of acceptable audit risk	–_____	–1 to –2
3.d.	**5-3-a**	Missing or unreasonable materiality judgment	–_____	–1
3.e.	**5-3-b**	Missing or unreasonable justification for materiality base and percentage	–_____	–1 to –2
3.f.	**5-4**	Missing or unreasonable tolerable misstatement allocations	–_____	–1
	5-1 to 5-4	Missing student's initials or date in top right corner of workpapers completed by student.	–_____	–1

Total points earned _____

Assignment 4 (10 points)

Student Name _____

Purpose of assignment

- To ensure you are familiar with the process of evaluating internal control and making preliminary assessments of control risk.

- To ensure you are able to design appropriate tests of controls and substantive tests of transactions.

Points allocation

			Your Points	Possible Deductions
		Total points possible (maximum point loss possible)	**10**	**−10**
Reqrmt.	W/P			
4.b. 4.c.	10-8	Incomplete or unreasonable control environment assessment	−_____	−1
4.d.	13-3	Incomplete or inaccurate internal control questionnaire	−_____	−1 to −2
4.e.	13-4	Incomplete or inaccurate control risk matrix	−_____	−1 to −2
4.f.	14-1	Incomplete or inappropriate design for tests of controls	−_____	−1 to −2
4.f.	14-2	Incomplete or inappropriate design for substantive tests of transactions	−_____	−1 to −2
	10-8, 13-1, 13-3, 13-4, 14-1, 14-2	Missing student's initials or date in top right corner of workpapers completed by student	−_____	−1

Total points earned _____

Assignment 5 (10 points)

Student Name _____

Purpose of assignment

To ensure you understand how to perform and evaluate tests of controls and substantive tests of transactions.

Points allocation

			Your Points	Possible Deductions
		Total points possible (maximum point loss possible)	**10**	**–10**

Reqrmt.	W/P		Your Points	Possible Deductions
5.c.	12-6	Missing or inaccurate listing of Computed Upper Exception Rates (CUER)	–_____	–1
5.h.	14-4	Incomplete or unreasonable conclusions, effects, or recommendations	–_____	–1 to –2
5.d, 5.e. 5.g.	14-7	Incomplete or inaccurate Sampling Data Sheet for Acquisitions	–_____	–1 to –3
5.f. 5.g.	14-8	Incomplete or inaccurate Sampling Exception Form for Acquisitions	–_____	–1 to –2
5.h.	93-2	Missing addition(s) to management letter	–_____	–1
	12-6, 14-3, 14-4, 14-7, 14-8, 93-2	Missing student's initials or date in top right corner of workpapers or audit program steps completed by student	–_____	–1

Total points earned _____

Assignment 6 — Option A (15 points)

Student Name _____

Purpose of assignment

To familiarize you with the audit procedures associated with the audit of accounts receivable.

To ensure you understand sampling procedures and concepts.

Points allocation

			Your Points	Possible Deductions
		Total points possible (maximum point loss possible)	**15**	**–15**
Reqrmt.	W/P			
6.i.	**21-1**	Missing or incomplete account receivable leadsheet	–_____	–1
6.h.	**21-2**	Missing or incorrect adjusting journal entry	–_____	–1
6.k.	**21-5**	Missing or inappropriate conclusion	–_____	–1
6.c.	**21-6**	Missing or incomplete Planned Tests of Balances Matrix	–_____	–1
6.d.	**21-17**	Incorrect calculation of sample size	–_____	–1
6.e.	**21-18**	Incomplete or incorrect sample selection	–_____	–1
6.f.	**21-19**	Incomplete or incorrect evaluations of confirmation responses	–_____	–1 to –3
6.g.	**21-20**	Incomplete or inaccurate misstatement projection figures	–_____	–1 to –2
6.g.	**21-21**	Incomplete or inappropriate decision, explanation, or conclusion	–_____	–1 to –2
6.j.	**21-21**	Incomplete or inaccurate calculation of unadjusted projected misstatement	–_____	–1
	21-1 to 21-3, 21-5, 21-6, 21-17 to 21-21	Missing student's initials or date in top right corner of workpapers completed by student	–_____	–1

Total points earned _____

Assignment 6 — Option B (15 points)

Student Name _____

Purpose of assignment

To familiarize you with the audit procedures associated with the audit of accounts receivable.

To ensure you understand sampling procedures and concepts.

Points allocation

			Your Points	Possible Deductions
		Total points possible (maximum point loss possible)	15	–15
Reqrmt.	W/P			
6.i.	21-1	Missing or incomplete account receivable leadsheet	–_____	–1
6.h.	21-2	Missing or incorrect adjusting journal entry	–_____	–1
6.k.	21-5	Missing or inappropriate conclusion	–_____	–1
6.c.	21-6	Missing or incomplete Planned Tests of Balances Matrix	–_____	–1
6.d.	21-22	Incorrect calculation of sample size	–_____	–1
6.e.	21-23	Incomplete or incorrect sample selection	–_____	–1
6.f.	21-24	Incomplete or incorrect evaluations of confirmation responses	–_____	–1 to –2
6.g.	21-25	Incomplete or inaccurate initial bounds	–_____	–1
6.g.	21-26, 21-27	Incomplete or inaccurate calculation of adjusted bounds	–_____	–1 to –2
6.g.	21-27, 21-28	Incomplete or inappropriate decision, explanation, or conclusion	–_____	–1 to –2
6.j.	21-28	Incomplete or inaccurate calculation of unadjusted projected misstatement	–_____	–1
	21-1 to 21-3, 21-5, 21-6, 21-22 to 21-28	Missing student's initials or date in top right corner of workpapers completed by student	–_____	–1

Total points earned _____

Assignment 6 — Option C (15 points)

Student Name _____

Purpose of assignment

To familiarize you with the audit procedures associated with the audit of accounts receivable.

To ensure you understand sampling procedures and concepts.

Points allocation

			Your Points	Possible Deductions
		Total points possible (maximum point loss possible)	**15**	**–15**

Reqrmt.	W/P		Your Points	Possible Deductions
6.i.	**21-1**	Missing or incomplete account receivable leadsheet	–_____	–1
6.h.	**21-2**	Missing or incorrect adjusting journal entry	–_____	–1
6.k.	**21-5**	Missing or inappropriate conclusion	–_____	–1
6.c.	**21-6**	Missing or incomplete Planned Tests of Balances Matrix	–_____	–1
6.d.	**21-29**	Incorrect calculation of sample size	–_____	–1
6.e.	**21-30**	Incomplete or incorrect sample selection	–_____	–1
6.f.	**21-31**	Incomplete or incorrect evaluations of confirmation responses	–_____	–1 to –2
6.g.	**21-31**	Incorrect calculation of projected misstatement	–_____	–1
6.g.	**21-32**	Missing or incorrect calculation of incremental allowance	–_____	–1
6.g.	**21-33**	Incorrect upper or lower misstatement limits	–_____	–1
6.g.	**21-33, 21-34**	Incomplete or inappropriate decision, explanation, or conclusion	–_____	–1 to –2
6.j.	**21-34**	Incorrect calculation of unadjusted projected misstatement	–_____	–1
	21-1 to 21-3, 21-5, 21-6, 21-29 to 21-34	Missing student's initials or date in top right corner of workpapers completed by student	–_____	–1
		Total points earned	_____	

Assignment 6 — Option D (15 points)

Student Name _____

Purpose of assignment

To familiarize you with the audit procedures associated with the audit of accounts receivable.

To ensure you understand sampling procedures and concepts.

Points allocation

			Your Points	Possible Deductions
		Total points possible (maximum point loss possible)	**15**	**–15**

Reqrmt.	W/P		Your Points	Possible Deductions
6.i.	**21-1**	Missing or incomplete account receivable leadsheet	–_____	–1
6.h.	**21-2**	Missing or incorrect adjusting journal entry	–_____	–1
6.k.	**21-5**	Missing or inappropriate conclusion	–_____	–1
6.c.	**21-6**	Missing or incomplete Planned Tests of Balances Matrix	–_____	–1
6.d.	**21-35**	Incorrect calculation of sample size	–_____	–1
6.e.	**21-36**	Incomplete or incorrect sample selection	–_____	–1
6.f.	**21-37**	Incomplete or incorrect evaluations of confirmation responses	–_____	–1 to –2
6.g.	**21-37**	Incorrect calculation of projected misstatement	–_____	–1
6.g.	**21-38**	Missing or incorrect calculation of precision interval	–_____	–1
6.g.	**21-39**	Incorrect upper or lower confidence limits	–_____	–1
6.g.	**21-39, 21-40**	Incomplete or inappropriate decision, explanation, or conclusion	–_____	–1 to –2
6.j	**21-40**	Incorrect calculation of unadjusted projected misstatement	–_____	–1
	21-1 to 21-3, 21-5, 21-6, 21-35 to 21-40	Missing student's initials or date in top right corner of workpapers completed by student	–_____	–1

Total points earned _____

Assignment 7 (15 points)

Student Name _____

Purpose of assignment

To familiarize you with the audit procedures associated with the audit of accounts payable.

Points allocation

			Your Points	Possible Deductions
		Total points possible (maximum point loss possible)	**15**	**−15**
Reqrmt.	W/P			
7.i.	**30-1**	Missing or incomplete accounts payable leadsheet	−_____	−1
7.h.	**30-2**	Missing or incorrect adjusting journal entry(ies)	−_____	−1 to −2
7.k.	**30-4, 30-5**	Missing initials, workpaper references, or conclusion on accounts payable audit program	−_____	−1
7.e.	**30-21**	Incomplete or incorrect sample selection	−_____	−1 to −3
7.f.	**30-22**	Incorrect summary of misstatements	−_____	−1 to −2
7.g.	**30-22**	Incorrect calculation of projected misstatement	−_____	−1
7.g.	**30-22**	Incorrect calculation of allowance for sampling error	−_____	−1
7.g.	**30-23**	Incomplete or inappropriate decision, explanation, or conclusion	−_____	−1 to −2
7.j.	**30-23**	Incomplete or inaccurate calculation of unadjusted projected misstatement	−_____	−1
	30-1, 30-2, 30-4, 30-5, 30-21, 30-22, 30-23	Missing student's initials or date in top right corner of workpapers completed by student	−_____	−1
		Total points earned	_____	

Assignment 8 (8 points)

Student Name _____

Purpose of assignment

To familiarize you with the audit procedures associated with the audit of cash.

Points allocation

			Your Points	Possible Deductions
		Total points possible (maximum point loss possible)	**8**	**–8**

Reqrmt.	W/P		Your Points	Possible Deductions
8.c.	**20-6**	Missing tickmarks on bank reconciliation	–_____	–1
8.c.	**20-6**	Missing tickmark explanations in tickmark legend	–_____	–1
8.d.	**20-8**	Missing tickmarks on schedule of interbank transfers	–_____	–1
8.d.	**20-8**	Missing tickmark explanation in tickmark legend	–_____	–1
8.e.	**20-2 to 20-4**	Missing initials, workpaper references, or conclusion on cash audit program	–_____	–1 to –2
8.f.	**20-1**	Missing or incomplete cash leadsheet	–_____	–1
	20-1 to 20-4, 20-6 to 20-8	Missing student's initials or date in top right corner of workpapers completed by student	–_____	–1

Total points earned _____

Assignment 9 (10 points)

Student Name _____

Purpose of assignment

To familiarize you with the audit procedures associated with the audit of inventory.

Points allocation

			Your Points	Possible Deductions
		Total points possible (maximum point loss possible)	10	–10

Reqrmt.	W/P			
9.i.	22-1	Missing or incomplete inventory leadsheet	–_____	–1
9.h.	22-6, 22-7	Missing initials, workpaper references, or conclusion on inventories audit program	–_____	–1
9.c.	22-15	Incomplete or incorrect sample selection	–_____	–1
9.c.	22-15	Incomplete or incorrect evaluation of test count tracing	–_____	–1
9.d.	22-18	Incorrect summary of misstatements	–_____	–1 to –2
9.e.	22-18	Incorrect calculation of projected misstatement and allowance for sampling error	–_____	–1
9.e., 9.f.	22-19, 22-20	Incomplete or inappropriate decision, explanation, or conclusion	–_____	–1 to –2
	22-1, 22-6, 22-7, 22-15, 22-18, 22-19, 22-20	Missing student's initials or date in top right corner of workpapers completed by student	–_____	–1

Total points earned _____

Assignment 10 (10 points)

Student Name _____

Purpose of assignment

To familiarize you with the audit procedures performed during the final phase of the audit process.

Points allocation

			Your Points	Possible Deductions
		Total points possible (maximum point loss possible)	**10**	**–10**

Reqrmt.	W/P		Your Points	Possible Deductions
10.c.	**1-1 to 1-5**	Financial statements and notes to financial statements not updated to reflect the adjustments made in trial balance	–_____	–1
10.c.	**3-1 to 3-3**	Missing or inaccurate adjustments; columns on trial balance not updated to reflect adjustments	–_____	–1
10.d.	**90-1**	Missing or incorrect figures	–_____	–1 to –2
10.d.	**90-1**	Missing or incorrect conclusion	–_____	–1
10.f.	**93-2**	Additional item not added to management letter	–_____	–1
10.e.	**Report**	Missing or incorrect report title	–_____	–1
10.e.	**Report**	Incorrect wording or structure of the audit report	–_____	–1 to –2
10.e.	**Report**	Missing or incorrect date and signature on report	–_____	–1
	1-1 to 1-5, 3-1 to 3-3, 90-1, 93-2	Missing student's initials or date in top right corner of workpapers completed by student	–_____	–1
		Total points earned	_____	

Oceanview Marine Company
Balance Sheet
December 31, 2007

ASSETS	2007	2006	2005
Current Assets			
Cash	$1,320,096	$1,089,978	$1,200,347
Accounts receivable: net (Notes 2 and 5)	**1,615,613**	1,285,593	1,180,982
Inventories (Notes 1(a), 3, and 5)	**13,552,200**	12,356,400	11,461,231
Prepaid expenses	17,720	15,826	15,275
Deposits	7,916	5,484	4,329
Total Current Assets	**16,513,545**	14,753,281	13,862,164
Property, Plant, and Equipment (Notes 1(b) and 4)			
At cost, less accumulated depreciation	596,517	612,480	627,771
TOTAL ASSETS	**$17,110,062**	$15,365,761	$14,489,935
LIABILITIES			
Current Liabilities			
Note payable -- Bank (Note 5)	$5,100,000	$4,250,000	$4,000,000
Accounts payable	**1,780,932**	1,403,247	1,106,574
Accrued liabilities	257,800	217,003	211,250
Federal income taxes payable	35,284	45,990	39,725
Current portion of long-term debt (Note 6)	5,642	5,642	5,642
Total Current Liabilities	**7,179,658**	5,921,882	5,363,191
Long-term Liabilities			
Long-term debt (Note 6)	409,824	415,466	421,108
TOTAL LIABILITIES	**7,589,482**	6,337,348	5,784,299
STOCKHOLDERS' EQUITY			
Common stock (Note 7)	10,000	10,000	10,000
Additional paid-in capital	2,500,000	2,500,000	2,500,000
Retained earnings	**7,010,580**	6,518,413	6,195,636
Total Stockholders' Equity	**9,520,580**	9,028,413	8,705,636
TOTAL LIABILITIES AND			
STOCKHOLDERS' EQUITY	**$17,110,062**	$15,365,761	$14,489,935

The accompanying notes form an integral part of these financial statements

Oceanview Marine Company
Statement of Income and Retained Earnings
December 31, 2007

	2007	2006	2005
Sales	**$26,460,237**	$22,889,060	$20,950,521
Sales returns and allowances	**39,874**	27,740	28,753
Net sales	**26,420,363**	22,861,320	20,921,768
Cost of sales	19,133,299	16,530,114	15,176,410
Gross profit	**7,287,064**	6,331,206	5,745,358
EXPENSES			
Accounting	48,253	46,750	44,610
Advertising	**30,874**	27,947	24,654
Depreciation	46,415	46,578	41,538
Bad debts	**179,958**	162,344	147,629
Business publications	1,231	872	115
Cleaning services	15,817	12,809	11,620
Fuel	64,161	53,566	41,593
Garbage collection	4,870	4,674	5,650
Insurance	16,415	16,303	16,144
Interest	427,362	364,312	356,829
Legal	69,752	29,914	22,654
Licensing and certification fees	33,580	27,142	24,148
Linen service	3,044	1,939	2,393
Medical benefits	4,178	4,624	4,287
Miscellaneous	47,739	16,631	25,430
Office supplies	26,390	23,289	21,462
Payroll benefits	569,110	461,214	430,688
Pension expense	40,770	37,263	18,900
Postage and courier	8,623	20,962	22,511
Property taxes	3,978	27,947	26,144
Rent	158,526	120,000	112,846
Repairs and maintenance	51,316	26,439	26,519
Salaries and wages	4,310,281	3,970,092	3,703,580
Security	96,980	100,098	93,800
Telephone	5,707	7,092	8,611
Travel and entertainment	21,633	16,303	14,952
Utilities	63,329	41,919	40,827
Total Expenses	**6,350,292**	5,669,023	5,290,134
Net income before income tax	**936,772**	662,183	455,224
Income tax expense	344,605	239,406	199,631
NET INCOME	**592,167**	422,777	255,593
Retained earnings at beginning of year	6,518,413	6,195,636	6,040,043
Less: Dividends	100,000	100,000	100,000
Retained earnings at end of year	**$7,010,580**	$6,518,413	$6,195,636

The accompanying notes form an integral part of these financial statements

Oceanview Marine Company
Statement of Cash Flows
December 31, 2007

	2007	2006	2005
Cash flows from operating activities			
Net income	**$592,617**	$422,777	$255,593
Adjustments to reconcile net income to net cash			
from operating activities:			
Depreciation of property, plant, and equipment	46,415	46,578	41,538
Decrease (increase) in accounts receivable	**(330,020)**	(104,611)	46,524
(Increase) in inventories	**(1,195,800)**	(895,169)	(562,215)
Decrease (increase) in prepaid expenses and deposits	(4,326)	(1,706)	2,347
Increase in accounts payable	**377,865**	296,673	223,827
Increase in accrued liabilities	40,797	5,753	7,923
Increase (decrease) in federal income taxes payable	(10,706)	6,265	7,851
Increase in note payable -- bank	850,000	250,000	200,000
Net cash provided by operating activities	366,212	26,560	223,388
Cash flows from financing activities			
Repayment of long-term debt	(5,642)	(5,642)	(5,642)
Dividends	(100,000)	(100,000)	(100,000)
Net cash used in financing activities	(105,642)	(105,642)	(105,642)
Cash flows from investing activities			
Acquisition of long-term assets	(30,452)	(31,287)	(29,835)
Net increase (decrease) in cash	230,118	(110,369)	87,911
Cash at beginning of year	1,089,978	1,200,347	1,112,436
Cash at end of year	$1,320,096	$1,089,978	$1,200,347

The accompanying notes form an integral part of these financial statements

1. Significant accounting policies

a. Inventories are recorded at the lower of cost or net realizable value.
    The perpetual inventory method is used to account for cost of goods sold.

b. Long-term assets are recorded at cost.
    Long-term assets are depreciated as follows:

	Rate	Method
Automobiles	30%	declining balance
Equipment	20%	declining balance
Office equipment	20%	straight-line
Building	4%	straight-line

On trade-ins, no gain or loss is recorded on disposal where a similar property is acquired.
A half-year of depreciation is recorded in the year of acquisition and the year of disposal.

2. Accounts receivable

	2007	2006	2005
Accounts receivable -- December 31	**$1,763,955**	$1,402,229	$1,297,618
Allowance for bad debts	**-148,342**	-116,636	-116,636
Accounts receivable -- net	**$1,615,613**	$1,285,593	$1,180,982

3. Inventories

	2007	2006	2005
Boats	$13,167,170	$12,030,247	$11,187,449
Repair parts	200,390	182,983	178,855
Supplies	156,789	143,170	94,927
	$13,524,349	$12,356,400	$11,461,231

4. Long-term assets -- net

	2007	2006	2005
	undepreciated balance	undepreciated balance	undepreciated balance
Land	$100,000	$100,000	$100,000
Automobiles	10,907	8,597	15,681
Equipment	83,467	84,008	71,186
Office equipment	25,291	25,495	28,996
Building	376,852	394,380	411,908
Docks	0	0	0
	$596,517	$612,480	$627,771

5. Notes payable -- Bank

The company has a revolving line of credit with First National Bank for up to $6,500,000.
The line of credit is secured by general assignment of accounts receivable and
inventory with interest payable monthly at prime plus 1%.
At December 31, 2007, the company had drawn $5,100,000 from this line of credit.
The interest rate was 9.5%.

6. Long-term debt

	2007	2006	2005
Ending balance	$415,466	$421,108	$426,750
Payments due within one year	-5,642	-5,642	-5,642
Long-term portion	$409,824	$415,466	$421,108

In 1993, the company entered into an agreement whereby Southeastern Enterprises
acquired 30% ownership in the company and also advanced the company a loan of $564,200.
The required annual payment of principal is $5,642. Interest on the outstanding balance is
payable monthly at the bank prime rate. If Southeastern Enterprises ceases to be a
shareholder, any remaining balance is due and payable in three years.

7. Stockholders' capital

	2007	2006	2005
Authorized:			
50,000 common shares $1 par value			
Issued:			
10,000 common shares	$10,000	$10,000	$10,000

8. Comparative figures

The comparative figures are based upon financial statements that were reported on
by other auditors.

9. Contingent liability

A customer bought a boat from the company that subsequently sank.
No injuries or death were reported. The customer has made a claim against the company.
The incident is being investigated and the company has not admitted liability.
No estimate of any liability can be made.

Oceanview Marine Company
Ratio Analyses
December 31, 2007

LIQUIDITY RATIOS:	Unadjusted 12/31/07	12/31/06	CHANGE	PERCENT CHANGE	INDUSTRY AVERAGE
Current ratio					
current assets / current liabilities	2.31	2.49	-0.18	-7.23%	1.21
Quick ratio					
(current assets – inventory) / current liabilities	0.42	0.40	0.02	5.00%	0.35
Sales / Receivables					
net sales / net ending receivables	16.05	17.78	-1.73	-9.73%	23.42
Number of days sales in A/R					
net ending receivables / (net sales / 365)	22.74	20.53	2.21	10.76%	15.58
Inventory turnover					
cost of sales / average inventory	1.48	1.39	0.09	6.47%	1.29
PROFITABILITY/PERFORMANCE RATIOS:					
Gross profit margin (%)					
gross profit / net sales	**27.58%**	**27.69%**	**-0.11%**	**-0.40%**	23.11%
Income before taxes / Owners' equity					
net income before taxes / total owners' equity	**0.10**	**0.07**	**0.03**	**42.86%**	0.07
Income before taxes / Total assets					
net income before taxes / total assets	**0.06**	**0.04**	**0.02**	**50.00%**	0.04
Sales / Long-term assets					
net sales / net long-term assets	**44.29**	**37.33**	**6.96**	**18.64%**	7.56
Sales / Total assets					
net sales / total assets	**1.54**	**1.49**	**0.05**	**3.36%**	1.39
Sales / Working capital					
net sales / (current assets – current liabilities)	**2.82**	**2.59**	**0.23**	**8.88%**	2.11
SOLVENCY RATIOS:					
Owners' Equity / Total assets					
total stockholders' equity / total assets	0.56	0.59	-0.03	-5.08%	0.28
Long-term assets / Owners' equity					
net long-term assets / total stockholders' equity	0.06	0.07	-0.01	-14.29%	0.54
Current liabilities / Owners' equity					
current liabilities / total stockholders' equity	0.75	0.66	0.09	13.64%	1.29
Total Liabilities / Owners' equity					
total liabilities / total stockholders' equity	0.79	0.70	0.09	12.86%	2.58

(**Note to instructor:** Because this workpaper is prepared early in the audit, the 2007 ratios are based on the unadjusted 2007 financial statement balances.)

Liquidity:

Although the liquidity ratios do not indicate there are any serious problem areas, they do reveal some possible warning signs:

- *The current ratio has declined by over 7% during the year. However, it is still above the 2:1 level, which is considered acceptable, and is nearly double the industry average.*

- *The collection period for accounts receivable increased by almost 11% and is much longer than the industry average. We should review with the client its credit policy and discuss the potential impact should the economy slow down -- the company could suffer major losses if customers cannot pay or if the company's cash flow worsens.*

Profitability:

The majority of the profitability ratios show stability or improvement over the previous year, and exceed industry averages. Although gross profit as a percentage of sales has dropped slightly, this should not be a concern since income before taxes as a percentage of owners' equity and total assets has improved slightly.

Solvency:

The solvency ratios have deteriorated somewhat:

- *Long-term Assets to Owners' Equity dropped nearly 15%, while the ratios of current and total liabilities to owners' equity have been increasing. This could be a concern if these trends continue in future years. In addition, the Long-term Assets to Owners' Equity ratio is significantly lower than the industry average.*

A. Identify ratios and trends, if any, that cause concern about the client's ability to continue as a going concern.

- **Collection period for accounts receivable has increased by over 10%.**

- **Long-term assets to owners' equity ratio is significantly lower than the industry average and is declining, while the liabilities to owners' equity ratios are increasing.**

- **Industry is cyclical, and quick ratio is low due to significant amount of inventory.**

- **There was a significant increase in legal costs from the prior year.**

B. Identify ratios and trends, if any, that indicate a high likelihood that the client will continue successfully as a going concern.

- **Sales have been steadily increasing, as have sales ratios.**

- **Income to owners' equity ratio and income to total assets ratio have been increasing.**

- **Current ratio and quick ratio are above industry averages. Although the current ratio has declined from the prior year, it is still above the benchmark of 2:1.**

C. Assess the client's financial condition as one of the following (check one)

☑ High probability that the company will successfully continue in business for at least two years and be able to pay its debts as they become due.

☐ Moderate possibility that the company will *not* successfully continue in business for at least two years and will be unable to pay its debts as they become due.

☐ High probability that the company will *not* successfully continue in business for at least two years and will be unable to pay its debts as they become due.

D. Briefly explain the reasoning behind your assessment.

There are no indications of impending financial difficulties.

Preliminary Analytical Procedures:
Identification of Accounts with Unexpected Fluctuations
December 31, 2007

Instructions: In the space provided below, identify those accounts that you believe are most likely to be *materially* misstated. The likelihood of misstatement may be indicated by an unexpected fluctuation, or lack of fluctuation where one is expected. Materiality reflects the size of the potential misstatement in relation to net income and other financial statement measures. Include your evaluation as to why the account balance differs from your expectations.

Balance Sheet Accounts: Identify balance sheet accounts that you believe are most likely to be misstated, and evaluate why the fluctuation (or lack thereof) is significant.

Account	2007 Bal.	2006 Bal.	Evaluation
Allowance for bad debts	*116,636 CR*	*116,636 CR*	*Allowance for bad debts is based on ending A/R balance. Ending A/R balance increased by over 360,000 from prior year, but allowance for bad debts remained constant.*
Accounts receivable	**1,762,682**	**1,402,229**	**Although sales have increased, the increase in sales cannot account for the entire increase in AR. AR represents 24 days sales (AR*365)/Sales in 2007 and 22 days sales in 2006. However, 2-day increase in sales is only $145,000 ((sales/365)x2), not 360,000.**
Federal income taxes payable	**35,284**	**45,990**	**Federal income taxes payable decreased while income before taxes and federal income taxes increased.**

Income Statement Accounts: Identify income statement accounts that you believe are most likely to be misstated, and evaluate why the fluctuation (or lack thereof) is significant.

Account	2007 Bal.	2006 Bal.	Evaluation
Property taxes	**3,978**	**27,947**	**Property taxes decreased significantly from prior year, without a corresponding decrease in the building or land accounts. This decrease should be investigated.**
Bad debts	**148,252**	**162,344**	**Bad debts expense decreased from prior year, while ending A/R increased. This could be investigated in conjunction with the allowance for bad debts account.**
Utilities, repairs and maintenance, legal service, and miscellaneous	**various**	**various**	**All of these expense accounts have increased significantly from the prior year and should be investigated.**

2-4-b
XX 2/19/08

Divisional Income Statement Accounts: Identify three divisional income statement accounts that you believe are most likely to be misstated, and evaluate why the fluctuation (or lack thereof) is significant.

Account & Division	2007 Bal.	2006 Bal.	Evaluation
Miscellaneous expense (new boats division)	**39,157**	**9,092**	**The new boats division showed a significant increase in miscellaneous expense that was not consistent with other divisions. This should be investigated.**
Wages—mechanics (repairs division)	**264,583**	**210,317**	**Mechanics' wages increased, but there was no corresponding increase in revenue for the repairs division. The source of the increase in wages should be investigated.**
Property taxes and bad debts expense (all divisions)	**various**	**various**	**Property taxes and bad debts decreased in all divisions. These should be investigated.**

(**Note to instructor:** Students may identify additional accounts that contain significant fluctuations.)

Account:	**Current Unadjusted Balance:**	**Prior Year's Audited Balance:**
Sales	$ 26,456,647	$ 22,889,060

Nature of potential misstatement:	*Sales may be overstated, possibly from either (1) fictitious sales being recorded in 2007 or (2) cutoff errors if the sales journal were held open past year-end.*

Client Explanation:	*Strong increase in sales in last quarter of 2007.*

Effect on audit procedures (be specific):	*Review sales recorded in last quarter of 2007 for fictitious sales.* *Increase extent of cutoff testing to determine whether any sales which occurred in January 2008 were recorded in December 2007 (cutoff errors).*

Account:	**Current Unadjusted Balance:**	**Prior Year's Audited Balance:**
Bad debts expense	$ 148,252	$ 162,344

Nature of potential misstatement:	**Bad debts expense may be understated if the client used an unreasonably small percentage in the calculation of the Allowance for Bad Debts.**

Client Explanation:	*Fewer accounts were written-off due to new policy to expend greater effort on collection of past due accounts.*

Effect on audit procedures (be specific):	**Review aging of accounts receivable to assess effectiveness of new collection policy. Test subsequent collections on past due receivables to assess reasonableness of percentages used to determine allowance and related bad debt expense.**

Account:	Current Unadjusted Balance:	Prior Year's Audited Balance:
Legal service	$ 69,752	$ 29,914

Nature of potential misstatement: **Legal service expense may be overstated.**

(Regarding the new lawsuit, if loss of lawsuit is probable and amount of loss can be estimated, accrual will need to be made for the liability.)

Client Explanation: *New lawsuit initiated over a boat that sank in 2007.*

Effect on audit procedures (be specific): **Examine invoices for legal services.**

Inquire of Oceanview's attorneys regarding likelihood of losing the lawsuit.

Account:	Current Unadjusted Balance:	Prior Year's Audited Balance:
Repairs and maintenance	$ 51,316	$ 26,439

Nature of potential misstatement: **Repairs and maintenance expense may be overstated if the client expensed some repairs and maintenance costs which should have been capitalized.**

Client Explanation: *Repairs made to building during year.*

Effect on audit procedures (be specific): **Examine invoices for significant repairs made to building and assess whether any represent items that should be capitalized.**

Account	Description	Unadjusted Trial Balance		Adjustments		Income Statement		Balance Sheet	
1010	Petty cash	200						200	
1015	Bank - Payroll	2,000						2,000	
1020	Bank - General	1,317,896						1,317,896	
1100	Accounts receivable	1,762,682		**1,273**				**1,763,955**	
1110	Allowance for bad debts	116,636	CR	**31,706**	CR			**148,342**	CR
1205	Inventory - boats	13,167,170		**27,851**				**13,195,021**	
1210	Inventory – repair parts	200,390						200,390	
1215	Inventory – supplies	156,789						156,789	
1300	Prepaid expenses	17,720						17,720	
1400	Deposits	7,916						7,916	
1500	Land	100,000						100,000	
1510	Automobiles	42,772						42,772	
1511	Accum. deprec. - automobiles	31,865	CR					31,865	CR
1520	Equipment	134,919						134,919	
1521	Accum. deprec. - equipment	51,452	CR					51,452	CR
1530	Office equipment	49,028						49,028	
1531	Accum. deprec. - office equip.	23,737	CR					23,737	CR
1540	Building	525,840						525,840	
1541	Accum. deprec. - building	148,988	CR					148,988	CR
1550	Docks	21,000						21,000	
1551	Accum. deprec. – docks	21,000	CR					21,000	CR
2010	Accounts payable - trade	1,750,831	CR	**30,101**	CR			**1,780,932**	CR
2100	Wages and salaries payable	182,360	CR					182,360	CR
2110	Payroll withholdings payable	42,972	CR					42,972	CR
2200	Federal income taxes payable	35,284	CR					35,284	CR
2300	Interest payable	32,468	CR					32,468	CR
2400	Notes payable - bank	5,100,000	CR					5,100,000	CR
2500	L.T. debt - current portion	5,642	CR					5,642	CR
2710	Long-term debt	409,824	CR					409,824	CR
3100	Common stock	10,000	CR					10,000	CR
3200	Additional paid-in capital	2,500,000	CR					2,500,000	CR
3500	Retained earnings	6,518,413	CR					6,518,413	CR
3510	Dividends paid	100,000						100,000	

Account	Description	Unadjusted Trial Balance		Adjustments		Income Statement		Balance Sheet
4100	Sales revenue	26,456,647	CR	**3,590**	CR	**26,460,237**	CR	
4500	Sales returns and allowances	37,557		**2,317**		**39,874**		
5100	Cost of goods sold	19,133,299				19,133,299		
6010	Accounting fees	48,253				48,253		
6020	Advertising	28,624		**2,250**		**30,874**		
6050	Depreciation	46,415				46,415		
6100	Bad debts	148,252		**31,706**		**179,958**		
6120	Business publications	1,231				1,231		
6240	Cleaning service	15,817				15,817		
6530	Fuel	64,161				64,161		
6810	Garbage collection	4,870				4,870		
6820	Insurance	16,415				16,415		
6830	Interest	427,362				427,362		
7110	Legal	69,752				69,752		
7130	Licensing & certification fees	33,580				33,580		
7150	Linen service	3,044				3,044		
7230	Miscellaneous	47,739				47,739		
7420	Office supplies	26,390				26,390		
7560	Postage	8,623				8,623		
7580	Property taxes	3,978				3,978		
7620	Rent - warehouse	158,526				158,526		
7630	Repairs and maintenance	51,316				51,316		
7710	Security	96,980				96,980		
7810	Telephone	5,707				5,707		
7850	Travel and entertainment	21,633				21,633		
7980	Utilities	63,329				63,329		
9100	Salaries - management	401,809				401,809		
9110	Salaries - office	55,512				55,512		
9120	Salaries - Sales	2,660,806				2,660,806		
9200	Wages - Mechanics	264,583				264,583		
9210	Wages - Rental	100,312				100,312		
9220	Wages - Warehouse	827,259				827,259		

Account	Description	Unadjusted Trial Balance	Adjustments	Income Statement	Balance Sheet
9500	Payroll benefits	569,110		569,110	
9600	Medical benefits	4,178		4,178	
9610	Pension expense	40,770		40,770	
9900	Income tax expense	344,605		344,605	
	TOTAL DR	43,438,119		25,868,070	17,607,595
	TOTAL CR	43,438,119		26,460,237	17,015,428
	NET INCOME	624,850		592,167	

LILTS BERGER & ASSOCIATES

Certified Public Accountants

Ocean City, Florida 33140

October 30, 2007

Mr. Donald Phillips, President
36 Clearwater Lake Road
Ocean City, Florida 33140

Dear Mr. Phillips:

This letter is to confirm our understanding of the terms of our engagement as the auditors of Oceanview Marine Company for the year ended December 31, 2007.

We will audit the company's balance sheet for December 31, 2007, and the related statements of income, retained earnings, and cash flows for the year then ended. The purpose of our audit is to form an opinion as to whether these statements are fairly presented **in conformity with accounting principles generally accepted in the United States of America.** We will review the company's federal and state income tax returns for the fiscal year ended December 31, 2007. In addition, we will be available to consult with you concerning the tax effects of any transactions or changes in company policies.

Our audit will be conducted in accordance with auditing standards generally accepted in the United States of America. Accordingly, our audit opinion will be based on our examination, made on a test basis, of your records, documents, assets, and equities. We will not examine all transactions, assets, or equities in detail, and the examination should not be relied on to detect all errors, fraud, or illegal acts that may have taken place. Notwithstanding, should we discover material misstatements resulting from error, fraud, or illegal acts during our audit, they will be disclosed to you. Please note that management of the company has the primary responsibility for maintaining adequate accounting records, for the safeguarding of assets, and for the preparation of accurate financial statements.

The timing of our examination is scheduled for performance and completion as follows:

Begin fieldwork	December 15, 2007
Completion of fieldwork	March 15, 2008
Delivery of management letter	March 22, 2008
Delivery of audit report	March 29, 2008
Delivery of tax returns	March 29, 2008

It is agreed that your staff will provide assistance with the preparation of data and by providing documents and records as needed.

Our fees will be based on our standard hourly rates. Invoices will be submitted periodically as the work progresses and are payable upon presentation. Should we find any conditions that could significantly affect our initial estimated total fees of $16,000, we will notify you immediately.

If the above terms are acceptable, and the services outlined are in accordance with the company's requirements, please sign the copy of this letter in the space provided and return it to us.

Yours very truly,

Per: *Charles Ward*

Charles Ward, CPA
Partner

The services set out in the foregoing letter are in accordance with our requirements. The terms set out are acceptable to us and are hereby agreed to.

Per: *Donald Phillips*

Donald Phillips, President
Oceanview Marine Company
November 10, 2007

Oceanview Marine Company
Assessment of Inherent Risk
December 31, 2007

	YES or NO				Assessment of Inherent Risk High, Medium, or Low *
	Account balance based on estimates[1]	Susceptible to theft or manipulation	Complex or non-routine transactions or calculations	Large number of transactions	
Cash	N	Y	N	Y	H
Accounts Receivable	N	N	N	Y	M
Allowance for Bad Debts	Y	N	N	N	M
Inventory	N	Y	N	Y	H
Prepaid Expenses	N	N	N	N	L
Property, Plant, & Equipment	N	N	Y	N	M
Accounts Payable	N	N	N	Y	M
Accrued Liabilities	N	N	N	N	L
Notes Payable	N	N	N	N	L
Taxes Payable	N	N	Y	N	M
Long-term Debt	N	N	N	N	L
Other Liabilities	N	N	N	N	L
Common Stock	N	N	N	N	L
Owners' Equity	N	N	N	N	L
Revenue	N	N	N	Y	M
Expenses *(excluding items below)*	N	N	N	N	L
Bad debts	Y	N	N	N	M
Depreciation	Y	N	N	N	M

* Any accounts that have one or more YES answers should be assessed as medium or high inherent risk. If not, explain why.

[1] Includes significant concerns about the account balance's net realizable value.

A.   **Likelihood of Financial Difficulty** (check one)   Source W/P reference: **2-3**

    ☑   High probability that the company will successfully continue in business for at least two years and be able to pay its debts as they become due.

    ☐   Moderate possibility that the company will *not* successfully continue in business for at least two years and will be unable to pay its debts as they become due.

    ☐   High probability that the company will *not* successfully continue in business for at least two years and will be unable to pay its debts as they become due.

B.   **Extent of Reliance on Financial Statements** (check one)

    ☐   Statements are used primarily internally by management.

    ☑   Statements are used primarily by management to obtain normal business loans.

    ☐   Client is a widely-held public company, or other wide-spread external use is highly probable.

C.   **Management Integrity** (check one)

    ☑   Management has high integrity.

    ☐   Management has moderate integrity.

    ☐   Management has low integrity.

D.   **Other Considerations**

Client is considering going public in the near future.

First year audit.

Conclusion — Based on the preceding analysis, acceptable audit risk for this engagement is:

☐ Relatively high (not a "risky" client)

☑ Moderate/Normal

☐ Relatively low ("risky" client)

Justify/explain your conclusion

Oceanview is very stable financially and is currently private-held. However, Oceanview is considering going public soon, and this is the first year we have audited the client. Accordingly, acceptable audit risk will be set as moderate.

1. Planning data

	Current year (unaudited)	Prior year
Sales/revenue (net)	26,419,090	22,861,320
Expenses	6,316,336	5,669,023
Gross margin	7,285,791	6,331,206
Pre-tax income	969,455	662,183
Current assets	16,516,127	14,753,281
Current liabilities	7,149,557	5,921,882
Total assets	17,112,644	15,365,761
Materiality		50,000

2. Preliminary Judgment about Materiality

Measurement base (i.e., income, revenue, assets)	Percentage applied*	Preliminary materiality
$ 969,455 **Pre-tax income**	**7.5 %**	**$ 75,000 (rounded)**

* Materiality percentages:

Pre-tax income	5 – 10%
Assets	½ – 1%
Equity	½ – 5%
Revenue	½ – 1%
Gross profit	½ – 5%

These materiality factors are provided as guidelines only, and should be used only as an aid in the development of your professional judgment. The materiality level should represent the largest amount of a misstatement or group of misstatements that would not, in your judgment, influence or change a decision based on the financial statements.

Note to instructor: For preliminary materiality, any amount from 5 to 10% of pre-tax income of $969,455 ($48,473 to $96,946) is acceptable. Students are not expected to come up with the same materiality and reasons shown on the next page. If their acceptable audit risk (from workpaper 5-2-b) was low, then preliminary materiality should be toward the low end of the range; if their acceptable audit risk was high, then preliminary materiality should be toward the high end. You may also wish to point out to students that the acceptable range for materiality is likely to be lower for a public company based on guidance from the SEC.

3. Justify/Support your Preliminary Judgment about Materiality

State the factors you considered when you chose the base and the percentage for the preliminary judgment about materiality. Link the percentage you chose to the level of acceptable audit risk.

Base:

Pre-tax income for the current year is considered representative; accordingly, pre-tax income was used as the materiality base as prescribed by our firm's policy.

Note to instructor: Because of the increase in net income for the current year compared to the prior year, some students may use an average of net income for the past three years, while others will select another base.

Percentage:

Since the acceptable level of audit risk is moderate, the middle of the percentage range (7.5%) was chosen.

Oceanview Marine Company
Allocation of Materiality:
Tolerable Misstatements
December 31, 2007

Account Name	2007 Unadjusted Trial Balance	Tolerable Misstatement
Cash	1,320,096	*20,000*
Accounts receivable	1,762,682	**30,000**
Allowance for bad debts	116,636CR	**15,000**
Inventory	13,524,349	*50,000*
Prepaid expenses	17,720	*2,000*
Deposits	7,916	*1,000*
Land	100,000	*-0-*
Automobiles	42,772	**1,000**
Equipment	134,919	*3,000*
Office equipment	49,028	*1,000*
Building	525,840	*10,000*
Accumulated depreciation	256,042CR	*5,000*
Accounts payable	1,750,831CR	**30,000**
Accrued liabilities	257,800CR	**15,000**
Federal income taxes payable	35,284CR	*5,000*
Notes payable – bank	5,100,000CR	**15,000**
Current portion of long-term debt	5,642CR	*1,000*
Long-term debt	409,824CR	*10,000*
Common stock	10,000CR	*1,000*
Additional paid-in capital	2,500,000CR	*10,000*

Combined tolerable misstatement (total of column 3)	**225,000**
Preliminary judgment about materiality (from w/p 10-3-a)	**75,000**
Multiply preliminary judgment by 3	x 3.00
Total (combined tolerable misstatement must be less than this total)	**225,000**

Note to instructor: Students are not expected to come up with the same tolerable misstatements as those shown above, as any tolerable misstatement which falls within the guidelines found in the policy statement is acceptable. Check to make sure that students' combined tolerable misstatement does not exceed three times their materiality level. Some students may not allocate the entire amount of tolerable misstatement available; we encourage them to allocate the full amount.

	Level of Control		
1. General:	**Strong**	**Weak**	**Comments**
Management's philosophy and operating style	✓		**W/P 10-1**
Organizational structure	✓		**W/P 10-1, 10-2**
Methods to communicate the assignment of authority and responsibility	✓		**W/P 10-2**
Management audit control methods	✓		**W/P 10-2**
Audit committee		✓	**W/P 10-3**
Internal audit		✓	**W/P 10-3**
Personnel policies and procedures	✓		**W/P 10-3, 10-4**
External influences	✓		**W/P 10-4**
2. Computer Hardware and Systems Software	✓		*W/P 10-5*
3. Computer Software Applications	✓		*W/P 10-6*
4. IT Department		✓	*W/P 10-7*

Conclusions:

The control environment appears to be strong overall. Lack of an audit committee or internal audit function is not unusual for a client of this size. Although deficiencies exist in control over IT Department, they are also not unusual for a client of this size.

Oceanview Marine Company
Statistical Attributes Sampling Data Sheet:
Sales
December 31, 2007

Define the objective: *Evaluation of internal controls and the accounting system for sales.*

Define the population precisely: *Sales transactions that occurred between Jan. 1, 2007 and Dec. 31, 2007, inclusive.*

Define the sampling unit, organization of population items, and random selection procedures:
Sales transactions as identified by sales invoice number, recorded sequentially in the sales journal. Computer-generated random sample.

Description of Attributes	Planning				Actual Results		
	EPER	TER	ARACR	Sample Size	Sample Size	Number of Exceptions	CUER
1. Proper approval of customer credit information. (E)	1.50	8	10	48	55	2	**9.4**
2. Goods have been shipped to customer. (E)	1.00	7	10	55	55	0	**4.1**
3. Amount recorded in journal agrees with invoice total. (A)	1.50	7	10	55	55	0	**4.1**
4. Footings and extensions on the sales invoice are correct. (A)	1.50	8	10	48	55	0	**4.1**
5. Price(s) per unit on invoice agree with approved price list. (A)	1.50	8	10	48	55	0	**4.1**
6. Quantity(ies) on sales invoice agree with quantity(ies) on bill of lading and customer order. (A)	1.50	8	10	48	55	0	**4.1**
7. Proper accounts were debited and credited. (Cl)	2.00	8	10	48	55	1	**6.9**
8. Sales transaction recorded promptly after shipment. (T)	1.50	9	10	42	55	1	**6.9**

Audit Objective for Tests of Controls and Substantive Tests of Transactions:
Accuracy	Existence or occurrence
Classification	Posting & summarization
Completeness	Timing

Oceanview Marine Company

Audit Program:

Evaluation of Internal Control over Acquisitions

December 31, 2007

| 13-1 |
| XX 2/23/08 |

Part 1: Obtain an understanding of the client's internal controls

	Initials	Date	Comments or W/P Reference
1. Discuss the control environment, accounting system, and control activities with management and client personnel.	BC	1/28/08	—
2. Obtain and study client's policy and procedures manuals and examine documents and records used in accounting system.	BC	1/28/08	—
3. Observe control-related client activities over purchases and cash disbursements.	BC	1/28/08	—

Part 2: Document your understanding of the client's internal control

4. Prepare a flowchart of the accounting system for acquisitions, including document flow, processing, disposition of documents, and control activities.	BC	1/29/08	W/P 13-2
5. Complete the "Internal Control Questionnaire—Acquisitions".	XX	2/23/08	W/P 13-3

Part 3: Preliminary assessment of control risk

6. Using the information obtained above, complete the "Preliminary Assessment of Control Risk—Acquisitions" matrix.	XX	2/23/08	W/P 13-4

Oceanview Marine Company
Internal Control Questionnaire:
Acquisitions
December 31, 2007

13-3
XX 2/23/08

Control Objectives and Questions	*	YES	NO	REMARKS
(1) Are purchases transactions supported by approved purchase orders?	E	✓		
(2) Are documents cancelled to prevent re-use?	E	✓		**By Don**
(3) Are receiving reports prenumbered and properly accounted for?	Co	✓		**By Cynthia**
(4) Are receiving reports controlled in a manner that helps assure that all goods received are recorded?	Co	✓		
(5) Is there internal verification of the calculations, prices, and quantities on vendors' invoices?	A	✓		**By Ray**
(6) Does someone independent of the recording of purchases function verify that the proper accounts have been debited and credited for purchases transactions?	Cl	✓		**By Cynthia**
(7) Is there an independent comparison of dates on receiving reports to dates recorded in the voucher register?	T		✓	
(8) Is there a policy requiring recording of purchases on a daily basis as close to time of receipt of goods as possible?	T		✓	
(9) Is the voucher register independently footed and posted to the general ledger?	P	✓		**Done automatically by computer**
(10) Is an independent reconciliation of the accounts payable subsidiary records and the general ledger performed regularly?	P	✓		**Reconciled by Ray, reviewed by Cynthia**

* Audit Objective for Tests of Controls and Substantive Tests of Transactions:

Accuracy	**Existence or occurrence**
Classification	**Posting & summarization**
Completeness	**Timing**

Oceanview Marine Company
Preliminary Assessment of Control Risk:
Acquisitions
December 31, 2007

Objectives:	Existence/ occurrence	Completeness	Accuracy	Classification	Timing	Posting and Summarization
Existing Controls:						
1. Purchase transactions are supported by approved purchase orders.	✓					
2. Documents are cancelled to prevent re-use.	✓					
3. Receiving reports are prenumbered and properly accounted for.		✓				
4. Receiving reports are controlled to ensure that all goods received are recorded.		✓				
5. Internal verification of details on invoice.			✓			
6. Independent verification of account classification.				✓		
7. Voucher register is footed and posted by computer.						✓
8. Independent reconciliation of A/P subsidiary records and general ledger performed regularly.						✓
9.						
Control Deficiencies:						
1. No independent comparison of dates on receiving reports to dates recorded in voucher register.					✓	
2. No company policy requiring recording of purchases as close to time of receipt of goods as possible.					✓	
3.						
4.						
Preliminary assessment of control risk: Enter H (high), M (medium), or L (low) in each column	L	L	L	L	H	L

Oceanview Marine Company
Audit Program (planning format):
Tests of Controls for Acquisitions
December 31, 2007

14-1
XX 2/23/99

Objectives	Existing Control(s)	Tests of Control(s)
Existence/occurrence— recorded acquisition transactions are for goods and services actually received	*Purchases transactions are supported by approved purchase orders (W/P 13-3, #1).* *Documents are cancelled to prevent re-use (W/P 13-3, #2).*	**Examine purchase orders for indication of approval.** **Examine voucher packages for indication of cancellation.**
Completeness—all acquisition transactions are recorded	*Receiving reports are prenumbered and accounted for regularly (W/P 13-3, #3).* *Receiving reports are controlled in a manner that helps assure that all goods received are recorded (W/P 13-3, #4).*	**Examine receiving reports for prenumbering and account for a sequence.** **Observe process of preparation and routing of receiving reports.**
Accuracy—acquisition transactions are recorded at the correct amounts	*Internal verification of invoice information (W/P 13-3, #5).*	**Examine vendor's invoices for indication of internal verification.**
Classification— acquisition transactions are debited and credited to the proper accounts	*Independent verification that the proper accounts have been debited and credited for purchases transactions (W/P 13-3, #6).*	**Inquire of Cynthia whether she periodically verifies that the proper accounts have been debited and credited for purchases transactions.**
Timing—acquisition transactions are recorded on the correct dates	*None.*	**N/A**
Posting and summarization— acquisitions are correctly totaled in the voucher register and posted to the G/L and subsidiary records	*Voucher register is independently footed and posted to the general ledger (W/P 13-3, #9).* *Independent reconciliation of A/P subsidiary records and the G/L performed regularly (W/P 13-3, #10).*	**Test computerized footing and posting of purchases transactions.** **Examine initials on the A/P account in the G/L indicating reconciliation.**

The Integrated Audit Practice Case

Suggested solutions

Oceanview Marine Company

Audit Program (planning format):

Substantive Tests of Acquisitions Transactions

December 31, 2007

| 14-2 |
| XX 2/23/08 |

Objectives	Substantive Tests of Transactions
Existence/occurrence— recorded acquisition transactions are for goods and services received	**Vouch from a sample of entries in the voucher register to the receiving reports to verify that goods have been received.**
Completeness—all acquisition transactions are recorded	**Trace from a sample of receiving reports to entries in the voucher register to verify that each acquisition of goods has been recorded.**
Accuracy—acquisition transactions are recorded at the correct amounts	**For a sample of entries in the voucher register:** **(1) compare amount recorded in register with total on vendor's invoice.** **(2) re-foot and re-extend the vendor's invoice.** **(3) compare prices per unit on invoice with vendor's catalog or price quote.** **(4) compare quantities on invoice with receiving report and purchase order.**
Classification— acquisition transactions are debited and credited to the proper accounts	**For a sample of entries in the voucher register, examine the vendor's invoice or other supporting document(s) to determine that the proper accounts were debited and credited.**
Timing—Acquisition transactions are recorded on the correct dates	**For a sample of acquisition transactions, compare the dates actually recorded with dates on supporting receiving reports.**
Posting and summarization— acquisitions are correctly totaled in the voucher register and posted to the G/L and subsidiary records	**Foot the voucher register and trace postings of totals to the purchases and accounts payable accounts in the general ledger.** **Trace a sample of individual entries from the voucher register to postings in the accounts payable subsidiary records.**

Oceanview Marine Company
Audit Program (performance format)
Tests of Controls and Substantive Tests of Transactions:
Acquisitions
December 31, 2007

14-3
XX 2/23/08

AUDIT PROCEDURES

	*	W/P	INIT	COMMENTS
1. Select a sample of _70_ voucher register (purchases journal) entries and for each entry:		*14-5*	**XX**	
a. review the purchase order for appropriate approval.	E	*14-7*	**XX**	*Attribute #2 on W/P 14-7*
b. vouch to the receiving report or other supporting document to ensure goods or services were received.	E	*14-7*	**XX**	*Attribute #3 on W/P 14-7*
c. compare amount recorded in voucher register with total on vendor's invoice.	A	*14-7*	**XX**	*Attribute #4 on W/P 14-7*
d. verify the mathematical accuracy of information on the vendor's invoice.	A	*14-7*	**XX**	*Attribute #5 on W/P 14-7*
e. compare quantity(ies) on invoice with quantiy(ies) on receiving report and purchase order.	A	*14-7*	**XX**	*Attribute #5 on W/P 14-7*
f. determine that all documents in voucher package are canceled (stamped "paid") to prevent re-use.	E	*14-7*	**XX**	*Attribute #6 on W/P 14-7*
g. review supporting documents to verify proper account classification.	Cl	*14-7*	**XX**	*Attribute #7 on W/P 14-7*
2. Select a sample of _70_ receiving reports and:				
a. trace each to the voucher register (purchases journal).	Co	*14-10*	BC	*No exceptions found.*
b. trace posting from voucher register to A/P subsidiary records.	P	*14-10*	BC	*No exceptions found.*
3. Determine by inspection that receiving reports are prenumbered, and are accounted for.	Co	*14-9*	BC	*No exceptions found.*
4. Test the accuracy of the footings in the voucher register, and trace postings of totals to the general ledger.	P	*14-9*	BC	*No exceptions found.*
5. Determine by inspection that an independent reconciliation of the A/P subsidiary records and the G/L is performed regularly.	P	*14-9*	BC	*No exceptions found.*

* **Audit Objective for Tests of Controls and Substantive Tests of Transactions:**

Accuracy	Existence or occurrence
Classification	Posting & summarization
Completeness	Timing

Oceanview Marine Company

Audit Program (performance format)
Tests of Controls and Substantive Tests of Transactions:
Acquisitions (continued)
December 31, 2007

14-4

XX 2/23/08

1.   **CONCLUSIONS:**

The preliminary assessment of control risk for the timing objective was high. Accordingly, controls over timing were not tested.

Based on unfavorable results of tests of attribute #2—approval of purchase orders— control risk for the Existence objective is increased to medium.

Results of substantive tests of transactions were favorable and support reduction of year-end substantive tests of balances.

2.   **EFFECT OF RESULTS ON AUDIT PLAN:**

Excepted as noted above, controls over purchases and accounts payable appear to be operating as documented and may be relied on.

3.   **RECOMMENDATIONS TO MANAGEMENT:**

- Remind client of importance of proper approval of acquisitions.

- Recommend client implement an internal control policy that encourages the timely recording of acquisitions.

Oceanview Marine Company
Non-statistical Attributes Sampling Data Sheet:
Acquisitions
December 31, 2007

Define the objective: *Evaluation of internal controls and the accounting system for acquisitions.*

Define the population precisely: *Purchase transactions that occurred between Jan. 1, 2007 and Dec. 31, 2007, inclusive.*

Define the sampling unit, organization of population items, and random selection procedures:
Purchase transactions as identified by voucher numbers recorded sequentially in voucher register. Computer-generated random sample.

Description of Attributes	Planning				Actual Results				
	EPER	TER	ARA-CR	Sample Size	Sample Size	Number of Exceptions	Sample Exception Rate	Estimated Sampling Error	CUER
1. Document package includes all documents appropriate for the transaction. (E)	1%	7%	10%	55	70	1	1.43%	4.0%	5.4%
2. Proper approval of purchase order. (E)	1%	8%	10%	48	70	3	4.29%	4.0%	8.3%
3. Goods have been received. (E)	1%	7%	10%	55	70	1	1.43%	4.0%	5.4%
4. Amount in voucher register agrees with amount on vendor's invoice. (A)	1%	7%	10%	55	70	1	1.43%	4.0%	5.4%
5. Quantities on vendor's invoice agree with related receiving report and P.O., and invoice is mathematically correct. (A)	1%	7%	10%	55	70	1	1.43%	4.0%	5.4%
6. All documents in voucher package have been stamped "paid". (E)	1%	8%	10%	48	70	1	1.43%	4.0%	5.4%
7. Proper accounts were debited and credited. (Cl)	1%	8%	10%	48	70	1	1.43%	4.0%	5.4%
8. Acquisitions recorded promptly after receipt of goods. (T)	3%	8%	10%	65	70	2	2.86%	4.0%	6.9%

Audit Objective for Tests of Controls and Substantive Tests of Transactions:
    Accuracy   Existence   Classification   Posting & summarization   Completeness   Timing

Oceanview Marine Company
Attributes Sampling Exception Form:
Acquisitions
December 31, 2007

This form is to be used to document the findings of tests of controls and substantive tests of transactions. In the column on the left, write the name and document number of each document tested. The numbers across the top of the matrix correspond to the "Description of Attributes" column on the Attributes Sampling Data Sheet.

For each document in column one, place an "X" in the column below the number of the attribute being tested by that document if there is an exception. Also use an "X" if one or more documents required to perform the test are missing (assuming the missing document(s) are applicable to the transaction). Leave it blank if there is no exception.

RECORD OF EXCEPTIONS

Identity of Item Selected	Attributes							
Document Number	1	2	3	4	5	6	7	8
Voucher 677								
1010							X	X
1409		X						
2280	X	X	X	X	X	X		X
3028		X						
65 additional items	0	0	0	0	0	0	0	0
Total Number of Exceptions	1	3	1	1	1	1	1	2
Total Sample Size	70	70	70	70	70	70	70	70

Account Number and Name		2007 Balance	Net Adjustments	2007 Adjusted Balance	2006 Balance	% Change (before adjustment)
1010 — Petty cash		200 *G/L*	**0**	**200**	200 *PY*	0.00%
1015 — Bank, payroll	*20-5*	2,000 *G/L*	**0**	**2,000**	2,000 *PY*	0.00%
1020 — Bank, general	**20-6**	1,317,896 *G/L*	**0**	**1,317,896**	1,087,778 *PY*	21.15%
	Total	1,320,096 *F*		**1,320,096**	1,089,978 *F*	21.11%

Tickmark legend

G/L   *Agreed to general ledger.*

PY   *Agreed to prior year's workpapers.*

F   *Footed without exception.*

AUDIT PROCEDURES

	*	W/P	INIT	COMMENTS

MODIFICATIONS TO AUDIT PROGRAM

	*	W/P	INIT	COMMENTS
1. Based on the results of previous audit procedures, complete appropriate modifications to this program.			*BC*	*As noted below.*

TESTS OF BALANCES—CASH ON HAND

	*	W/P	INIT	COMMENTS
2. In the presence of client, count petty cash fund, undeposited receipts, and other cash.	A E		*BC*	*Petty cash counted Dec. 31, 2007. No exceptions. Cynthia present.*
3. Obtain explanations of differences between the petty cash float and the cash count.	A		*BC*	*N/A. No difference.*
4. Note any IOUs, reused vouchers, or stale dated checks.	Co		*BC*	*None*
Other procedures:			*BC*	*None*

TESTS OF BALANCES—CASH IN BANK

	*	W/P	INIT	COMMENTS
5. Obtain cutoff bank statements *directly from the bank* for all bank accounts open at any time during the year per bank confirmation or company records.			*BC*	
6. Obtain bank confirmations, directly from the bank, for all accounts open at any time in the year.		*20-7*	*BC*	
7. Obtain year-end bank reconciliations for all accounts.	A E Co	*20-5* *20-6*	*BC*	
8. For each reconciliation, trace the balance per books to the general ledger.	A D	*20-5* *20-6*	*BC*	*Done for payroll and general bank account.*
9. Verify the arithmetic accuracy of each reconciliation.	A D	*20-5* **20-6**	*BC* **XX**	*Done for payroll bank acct.* **Done for general bank acct.**
10. For each reconciliation, trace the balance per bank (unadjusted) to the bank confirmation.	A E	*20-7*	*BC* **XX**	*Done for payroll bank acct.* **Done for general bank acct.**

* **Audit Objectives:**
  Accuracy **Classification** **Completeness** **Cut**off Detail tie-in **Existence**
  Presentation and disclosure **Rights and obligations**

AUDIT PROCEDURES

	*	W/P	INIT	COMMENTS
11. Trace checks over $ _1,000_ on cutoff statement to list of outstanding checks on year-end bank reconciliation.	A Cu E	20-5 **20-6**	BC **XX**	*Done for payroll bank acct.* **Done for general bank acct.**
12. Investigate checks over $ _1,000_ on the reconciliation that did not clear by the cutoff statement date.	A Co Cu	20-5 **20-6**	BC **XX**	*Done for payroll bank acct.* **Done for general bank acct.**
13. Trace all deposits-in-transit from bank reconciliation to cutoff statement(s).	A Cu E	20-5 **20-6**	BC **XX**	*N/A for payroll bank acct.* **Done for general bank acct.**
14. Trace all other items on bank reconciliation to books and/or bank account as appropriate. Trace all other items on bank statement to reconciliation or books as appropriate. Inquire about old or unusual items on reconciliation.	A E	20-5 20-6	BC	*No unusual items.*
15. Verify bank confirmation and inquire of management whether there are any restrictions preventing use of cash for current purposes.	P R	20-7	BC	*No restrictions.*
16. Perform tests of interbank transfers occurring within 10 days of year-end:	A Cu			
a. Determine that date per books for disbursing and receiving accounts are in the same period.	Co E	**20-8**	**XX**	**Disbursing and receiving dates per books are in same period.**
b. Trace any outstanding deposits or outstanding checks to bank reconciliation.		**20-8**	**XX**	**No exceptions.**
c. Trace dates and amounts to cash receipts and cash disbursements journals.		20-8	BC	*No exceptions.*
d. Trace dates and amounts to bank statements (cutoff statements for amounts after year-end).		**20-8**	**XX**	**No exceptions.**
Other Procedures:			BC	*None.*

* **Audit Objectives:**
Accuracy **Cl**assification **Co**mpleteness **Cu**toff **D**etail tie-in **E**xistence
Presentation and disclosure **R**ights and obligations

<u>**AUDIT PROCEDURES**</u>

ANALYTICAL PROCEDURES

	*	W/P	INIT	COMMENTS
17. Compare ending cash balances with other month-end balances and prior year(s). Obtain explanations and other evidence as appropriate to account for unexpected differences.	A Co E		BC	*Compared 2006 and 2007 month to month. No unusual variances other than those caused by normal sales cycles.*
Other procedures:			BC	*None*

STATEMENT PRESENTATION

	*	W/P	INIT	COMMENTS
18. Review groupings and compare to prior year. Reclassify credit balances as current liabilities. Consider re-classification for restricted or appropriated cash.	P		BC	*No credit balances. Classification is appropriate.*
Other procedures:			BC	*None*

CONCLUSION

19. State, in your opinion, if the cash reported in the financial statements is fairly presented and is in accordance with GAAP.

In our opinion, cash appears to be fairly stated in accordance with GAAP.

* **Audit Objectives:**
 Accuracy   Classification   Completeness   Cutoff   Detail tie-in   Existence
 Presentation and disclosure   Rights and obligations

Oceanview Marine Company
Bank Reconciliation – General Bank Account
December 31, 2007

Balance per bank statement			1,332,686.93	Balance per books, unadjusted	1,317,896.00
			20-7		**G/L 20-1**
Add: Deposits in transit:				Adjustments:	0.00
Dec. 30 '07	26,262.78	#			
Dec. 30 '07	12,346.98	#	38,609.76		
	F				
Deduct: Outstanding checks:					
5835 Nov. 02 '07	1,516.18	~			
5919 Nov. 23 '07	375.75				
6016 Dec. 07 '07	679.00				
6139 Dec. 21 '07	345.00				
6245 Dec. 28 '07	5,670.00	~			
6248 Dec. 28 '07	984.00				
6249 Dec. 28 '07	2,350.49	~			
6251 Dec. 28 '07	321.48				
6252 Dec. 28 '07	3,781.70	~			
6254 Dec. 28 '07	672.58				
6256 Dec. 28 '07	1,251.83	~			
6257 Dec. 28 '07	12,987.35	~			
6258 Dec. 28 '07	337.12				
6260 Dec. 28 '07	1,841.80	~			
6261 Dec. 28 '07	456.90				
6263 Dec. 28 '07	149.15				
6264 Dec. 28 '07	1,385.29	~			
6265 Dec. 28 '07	456.86				
6266 Dec. 28 '07	3,450.91	^			
6267 Dec. 28 '07	733.00				
6268 Dec. 28 '07	200.00				
6269 Dec. 28 '07	13,454.30 **20-8**		53,400.69		
	F	~			
Balance per bank, adjusted			1,317,896.00	Balance per books, adjusted	1,317,896.00
			F		**F**

Tickmark Legend

G/L *Agreed to general ledger balance.*

**Agreed to deposit on cutoff bank statement.**

~ **Agreed to check clearing with cutoff bank statement**

^ **Check did not clear with cutoff bank statement. Reviewed January 2008 bank statement; check cleared in January 2008.**

F **Footed without exception.**

_____**Oceanview Marine Company**_____
CUSTOMER NAME

[   ]

Financial
Institution's
Name and
Address

FIRST NATIONAL BANK
317 Fifth Avenue
Ocean City, Florida 33140

We have provided our accountants the following information as of the close of business on **December 31**, 20 **07**, regarding our deposit and loan balances. Please confirm the accuracy of the information, noting any exceptions to the information provided. If the balances have been left blank, please complete this form by furnishing the balance in the appropriate space below.* Although we do not request nor expect you to conduct a comprehensive, detailed search of your records, if during the process of completing this confirmation additional information about other deposit or loan balances comes to your attention, please include such information below. Please use the enclosed envelope to return the form directly to our accountants.

[   ]

1. At the close of business on the date listed above, our records indicated the following deposit balance(s):

ACCOUNT NAME	ACCOUNT NUMBER	INTEREST RATE	BALANCE*
Payroll	**010-123456**	**N/A**	$ **10,451.38** *20-5*
General	**030-987654**	**N/A**	$ **1,332,686.93 20-6**

2. We were directly liable to the financial institution for loans at the close of business on the date listed above as follows:

ACCOUNT NO./ DESCRIPTION	BALANCE*	DATE DUE	INTEREST RATE	DATE THROUGH WHICH INTEREST IS PAID	DESCRIPTION OF COLLATERAL
Line of credit	**$5,100,000** *32-1*	**Demand**	**9.5%**	**Dec. 8, 2007**	**Receivables and inventory**

Cynthia Rathberg
(Customer's Authorized Signature)

January 1, 2008
(Date)

The information presented above by the customer is in agreement with our records. Although we have not conducted a comprehensive, detailed search of our records, no other deposit or loan accounts have come to our attention except as noted below.

_____Robert Johnson_____
(Financial Institution Authorized Signature)

January 10, 2008
(Date)

_____Vice-President_____
(Title)

EXCEPTIONS AND/OR COMMENTS
None

Please return this form directly to our accountants: [*Lilts Berger & Associates*   ]
                                                                      100 Main Street
* Ordinarily, balances are intentionally left blank if they are not   *Ocean City, Florida 33140*
available at the time the form is prepared.   [   ]

Oceanview Marine Company
Schedule of Interbank and Intercompany Transfers
December 31, 2007

	Amount	Disbursing Account		Receiving Account	
		Date per Books	Date per Bank	Date per Books	Date per Bank
Transfer from general to payroll Check #6269	$13,454.30 **20-6** *	12/28/07 X	1/4/08 ✓✓	12/28/07 ∧	12/28/07 ✓
Transfer from general to payroll Check #6274	$10,000 *	1/4/08 X	1/7/08 ✓✓	1/4/08 ∧	1/6/08 ✓✓

Audit tickmark legend

* Traced and agreed payee, payor, check number, and check amount to the cash disbursements journal (no exceptions noted).

X Traced and agreed the disbursement date per books to the cash disbursements journal (no exceptions noted).

∧ Traced and agreed the receipt date per books to the cash receipts journal (no exception noted).

✓ Traced to year-end bank statement.

✓✓ **Traced to cutoff bank statement.**

Account Number and Name	2007 Balance	Net Adjustments		2007 Adjusted Balance	2006 Balance	% Change (before adjustment)
1100 — Accounts receivable *21-9*	1,762,682 *G/L*	**21-2**	**1,273**	**1,763,955**	1,402,229 *PY*	25.71%
1110 — Allowance for bad debts	− 116,636 *G/L*	**21-2**	**−31,706**	**−148,342**	− 116,636 *PY*	0.00%
Total	1,646,046 *F*			**1,615,613**	1,285,593 *F*	28.04%

Tickmark legend

G/L   *Agreed to general ledger.*

PY   *Agreed to prior year's workpapers.*

F   *Footed without exception.*

Oceanview Marine Company
Adjusting Journal Entries: Accounts Receivable
December 31, 2007

Account Number and Name	Debit	Credit
6100 — Bad debts expense	*$ 31,706.00*	
1110 — Allowance for bad debts		*$ 31,706.00*
		21-1

Explanation: To adjust allowance account to estimated balance at year-end.
Estimated allowance   21-15 $ 148,342
Per client's books $ 116,636

Account Number and Name	Debit	Credit
1100 — Accounts receivable – Underwood	**890.00**	
1100 — Accounts receivable – Steinbart	**2,700.00**	
4500 — Sales returns and allowances	**2,317.00**	
1100 — Accounts receivable – Howard		**117.00**
1100 — Accounts receivable – Meier		**2,200.00**
4100 — Sales		**3,590.00**

Explanation: To correct misstatements discovered during audit of accounts receivable. Net effect on accounts receivable is an increase of $1,273.

21-1

AUDIT PROCEDURES	*	W/P	INIT	COMMENTS
MODIFICATIONS TO AUDIT PROGRAM				
1. Based on the results of previous audit procedures, complete the Planned Tests of Balances Matrix for accounts receivables and, if necessary, make appropriate modifications to this audit program.		**21-6**	**XX**	*No modifications of audit program deemed necessary.*
TESTS OF BALANCES				
2. Obtain an aged listing of accounts receivable as of year-end and:		*21-7 to 21-9*	*BC*	*No exceptions.*
(a) foot the listing and crossfoot totals.	D			
(b) trace total of aged receivables to the general ledger.	D			
(c) trace entries for individual customers from the aging analysis to the individual accounts in the accounts receivable subsidiary records.	D			
3. Perform confirmations of accounts receivable. Verify by confirmation or alternative means all accounts selected for confirmation.	A E	**21-7 to 21-14**		
(a) determine sample size for confirmation testing.		**21-xx to 21-yy**	**XX**	
(b) select individual accounts for confirmation testing.			**XX**	
(c) evaluate differences between receivable balances and confirmation responses (or alternative procedures). Determine whether differences are valid timing differences or misstatements.			**XX**	
(d) generalize misstatements to the population of accounts receivable and evaluate acceptability of the population.			**XX**	
4. Review allowance for bad debts and:		*21-15 and 21-16*	*BC*	*Adjustments required as noted on W/P 21-2.*
(a) discuss with management whether the allowance amount is adequate.	A			
(b) review payments received after year end.	Co			
(c) prepare an analysis of the allowance account and compare to the general ledger.	Rv			

* **Audit Objectives:**
  Accuracy   **Cl**assification   **Co**mpleteness   **Cu**toff   **D**etail tie-in   **E**xistence
  Presentation and disclosure   **R**ealizable **v**alue   **R**ights and obligations

AUDIT PROCEDURES

	*	W/P	INIT	COMMENTS
5. Investigate any material credit balances and re-classify as accounts payable.	A P Ro		BC	*N/A. No credit balances.*
6. Review control account for unusual postings.	A Co		BC	*Reviewed for entire year. All entries appear to be routine.*
7. Physically inspect all notes receivable in the client's possession.	A Co Ro		BC	*N/A. None.*
8. Review minutes, agreements, and bank confirmation to determine if any accounts or notes have been assigned, pledged or discounted.	Ro	20-7	BC	*A/R pledged as security for bank loan.*
9. Review accounts receivable cut-off.	Cu		BC	*Last sales invoice #8801. Item was not in inventory listing.*
10. Trace subsequent receipts to outstanding accounts receivable.	A Co		BC	*No exceptions found.*
Other procedures:			BC	*None.*

ANALYTICAL PROCEDURES

	*	W/P	INIT	COMMENTS
11. Analyze the relationship between receivables and sales, and compare with relationships for the preceding year(s).	Rv		BC	*Differences not significant.*
12. Review the aged accounts receivable trial balance and compare to prior periods.	Rv	21-9	BC	*Differences not significant.*
13. Compare sales returns and allowances as a percentage of gross sales with previous years.	Rv		BC	*2007 — 0.1%* *2006 — 0.1% No difference.*
14. Compare individual customer balances over a stated amount with previous years.	Rv		BC	*N/A. Larger accounts are for boat sales that are not repeated by same customer from year to year.*
15. Compare bad debts as a percentage of net sales with previous years.	Rv	21-16	BC	*Differences not significant.*
16. Compare the number of days accounts receivable are outstanding with previous years.	Rv	2-1	BC	*Differences not significant.*

* Audit Objectives:
Accuracy   **Cl**assification   **Co**mpleteness   **Cu**toff   **D**etail tie-in   **E**xistence
Presentation and disclosure   **R**ealizable value   **R**ights and **o**bligations

AUDIT PROCEDURES

17. Compare aging categories as a percentage of accounts receivable with previous years.

18. Compare allowance for bad debts as a percentage of accounts receivable to previous years.

    Other procedures:

*	W/P	INIT	COMMENTS
Rv		BC	*Differences not significant.*
Rv	*21-16*	BC	*Difference not significant.*
		BC	*None*

STATEMENT PRESENTATION

19. Verify that any encumbrances are appropriately disclosed.

20. Verify that there is segregation of accounts and notes receivable and any long-term receivables.

21. Inquire whether there are any receivables from related parties.

    Other procedures:

*	W/P	INIT	COMMENTS
P		BC	*A/R pledged to bank. Note to financial statements required.*
C P		BC	*N/A. No long-term receivables.*
P		BC	*None. Inquired of Cynthia.*
		BC	*None*

CONCLUSION

22. State, in your opinion, if the notes and accounts receivable reported in the financial statements are fairly presented and are in accordance with GAAP.

> **(Options A and D): Based on the tests performed, accounts receivable appears to be fairly stated in accordance with GAAP.**
>
> **(Options B and C): After client corrected misstatements found during testing, accounts receivable appears to be fairly stated in accordance with GAAP.**

* **Audit Objectives:**
  Accuracy   Classification   Completeness   Cutoff   Detail tie-in   Existence
  Presentation and disclosure   Realizable value   Rights and obligations

Oceanview Marine Company
Planned Tests of Balances Matrix — Accounts Receivable
December 31, 2007

Audit Objectives	Acceptable Audit Risk (High, Medium or Low)	Inherent Risk (High, Medium, or Low)	Analytical Procedures (High, Medium, or Low potential for misstmts.)	Control Risk: Sales Cycle (High, Medium, or Low)	Substantive Tests of Transactions: Sales Cycle (High, Medium, or Low likelihood of misstmts.)	Planned Tests of Balances (Extensive, Medium, or Reduced Tests)	Comments *
Detail tie-in	H (M) L	H M (L)	H M (L)	H M (L)	H M (L)	E M (R)	
Existence	H (M) L	H (M) L	H M (L)	H (M) L	H M (L)	E (M) R	*Risk of improper revenue recognition per SAS 99.*
Completeness	H (M) L	H (M) L	H M (L)	H M (L)	H M (L)	E (M) R	*Incentive for private company to understate revenue.*
Accuracy	H (M) L	H (M) L	H M (L)	H M (L)	H M (L)	E (M) R	**Concern for large number of transactions.**
Classification	H (M) L	H M (L)	H M (L)	(H) M L	H M (L)	E (M) R	**Concern for lack of controls over sales classification.**
Realizable value	H (M) L	H (M) L	H (M) L	H (M) L	H M (L)	E (M) R	**Account based on estimates; AP raised concerns; weak controls over credit approval.**
Cutoff	H (M) L	H (M) L	H (M) L	H M (L)	H M (L)	E (M) R	**Inherent risk of misstatements; AP raised concerns.**
Rights	H (M) L	H (M) L	H M (L)	H M (L)	H M (L)	E M (R)	
Presentation and disclosure	H (M) L	H M (L)	H M (L)	H M (L)	H M (L)	E M (R)	

Preliminary judgment about materiality: $ _75,000_

Tolerable misstatement for accounts receivable: $ _30,000_

* For each audit objective with *extensive* or *medium* planned tests of balances (E or M in column seven), use column eight to indicate your primary concern(s) about that objective.

Oceanview Marine Company
Calculation of Sample Size: Non-statistical Sampling
December 31, 2007

Decisions and Facts for Determining Sample Size:

Book Value of the recorded population: *1,762,682.00 (86 accounts)*

Stratum 1: Book value of individually material accounts: *1,197,792.00 (14 accounts)*
(test **all** material accounts)

Stratum 2: Book value of all remaining accounts (BV): **564,890.00**
(test only a sample)

Tolerable Misstatement (TM): **30,000.00**

Assurance Factor (AF): *2.1* (from table below)

n (stratum 2): **40** (round to whole number)
Note: n = (BV x AF) / TM

Assurance Factor for Determining Sample Size:
(The assurance factor should be based on considerations of acceptable audit risk, inherent risk, control risk, results of preliminary analytical procedures, and the results of substantive tests of transactions)

Assurance Factors

Assessment of Inherent and Control Risk	Risk That Other Substantive Procedures Will Fail to Detect a Material Misstatement			
	Maximum	Slightly Below Maximum	Moderate	Low
Maximum	3.0	2.7	2.3	2.0
Slightly below maximum	2.7	2.4	2.0	1.6
Moderate	2.3	2.1	1.6	1.2
Low	2.0	1.6	1.2	1.0

Justify/explain your decision:

Inherent risks for the existence and accuracy objectives for accounts receivable were assessed as medium. After performing tests of transactions for the sales and cash receipts cycle, control risks for the existence and accuracy objectives for accounts receivable were assessed as medium and low, respectively. Acceptable audit risk is medium. Results of substantive tests of transactions and analytical procedures were generally favorable, but risk that other procedures will fail to detect a material misstatement was set slightly below maximum since this is a first year audit.

Other factors considered:

Little anticipated misstatement in accounts receivable.

Oceanview Marine Company
Sample Selection: Non-statistical Sampling
December 31, 2007

Audit Area: *Accounts receivable*

Stratum 1:	All accounts greater than tolerable misstatement of:	**30,000.00**

Stratum 2:	Sampling Interval = Number of Accounts / Sample Size =	**2**

(round **down** to whole number)

Stratum 1:	**Customer Name**	**Amount Confirmed**
1	*Anthony Underwriters*	*117,990.00*
2	**John Bischoff**	**113,655.00**
3	**Robert Borst**	**155,690.00**
4	**Dan Devine**	**121,456.00**
5	**Robert Geyer**	**68,904.00**
6 to 14	*Various*	*620,097.00*
	Total	**1,197,792.00**

Stratum 2:	**Customer Name** *(Random Starting Point: 1st account)*	**Amount Confirmed**
1	*James Abbott*	*21,345.00*
2	**Robert Allen**	**432.00**
3	**Mary Bates**	**340.86**
4	**Benson Realty**	**113.87**
5	**Rita Capicchoini**	**679.61**
6 to 35	*Various*	*292,641.14*
	Total	**315,552.48**

Stratum 1--Summary of Confirmation Differences:

Customer Name	A/R Balance per Client's Records	A/R Balance per Customer	Amount of Difference	Reason(s) for Difference	Amount of Client Misstatement, if any Over (Under)
Robert Borst	**155,690.00**	**0.00**	**155,690.00**	**Timing difference; not an exception.**	**0.00**
John Underwood	**46,770**	**47,660**	**-890.00**	**Transposition error by client.**	**-890.00**

Net misstatement in stratum 1: **-890.00**

Stratum 2—Summary of Confirmation Differences:

Customer Name	A/R Balance per Client's Records	A/R Balance per Customer	Amount of Difference	Reason(s) for Difference	Amount of Client Misstatement, if any Over (Under)
Richard Howard	**11,678.00**	**11,561.00**	**117.00**	**Client failed to issue credit memo.**	**117.00**
Diane Meier	**21,456.90**	**19,256.90**	**2,200.00**	**Pricing error on floor model.**	**2,200.00**
Paul Steinbart	**13,654.00**	**16,354.00**	**-2,700.00**	**Transposition error by client.**	**-2,700.00**

Net misstatement in stratum 2: **-383.00**

Calculation of Projected Misstatement:

Stratum 1 Projected Misstatement:

Net misstatement in stratum 1 = **-890.00**

(misstatements are not projected since tested 100%)

Stratum 2 Projected Misstatement:

(net misstatement in stratum 2/stratum 2 $ sample size) x (stratum 2 $ population size) = **-685.63**

Total projected misstatement = **-1,575.63**

Calculation of Actual Allowance for Sampling Error:

Tolerable misstatement = **30,000.00**

Less: Projected misstatement = **1,575.63**

Allowance for sampling error = **28,424.37**

Decision (check one):

      ☑   Accept population as stated.
           (No adjustment required for account to be fairly stated.)

      ☐   Request client adjust population.
           (Account is not fairly stated, but if client corrects misstatements found in sample, account
           will be acceptable.)

      ☐   Expand audit tests.
           (Account is not fairly stated, and cannot be made acceptable by correcting misstatements
           found in sample.)

      ☐   Some other action. Specify:

Explain/Justify your Decision:

**Projected misstatement, after allowing for sampling error, is sufficiently less than tolerable
misstatement to justify accepting the account as fairly stated.**

(**Note to instructor**: Some students may check the second box above, since they are asked to record an
adjustment for the actual errors detected)

Conclusion:

Based on the results of our tests, accounts receivable appears to be fairly stated.

Calculation of Unadjusted Projected Misstatement:

                        Projected misstatement = **-1,575.63**   **(understated)**

           Less: Adjusting journal entry (net) = **1,273.00**   **(increase)**

         Unadjusted projected misstatement = **-302.63**   **(understated)**
       (carry forward to *Summary of Possible Misstatements* (workpaper 90-1))

Oceanview Marine Company
Calculation of Sample Size: Monetary-Unit Sampling
December 31, 2007

Audit Area: *Accounts receivable*

Population: *Book value of accounts receivable $1,762,682*

Sampling Unit: *Dollars in accounts receivable at 12/31/07*

Decision and Facts for Determining Sample Size:

Book value of population =	*1,762,682*	
Acceptable risk of incorrect acceptance =	*30%*	*(medium)*
Tolerable misstatement =	**30,000**	
Average percent of misstatement assumption =	*100%*	
Estimated misstatement in the population =	*1,000*	*(overstated)*

Calculation of Tolerable Misstatement Rate and Estimated Population Misstatement Rate:

	Upper Bound	Lower Bound
(a) Tolerable misstatement =	**30,000**	**30,000**
(b) Average percent of misstatement assumption =	*100%*	*100%*
a / b =	**30,000**	**30,000**
Book value of population =	*1,762,682*	*1,762,682*
Tolerable misstatement rate = (round to nearest percent)	**2%**	**2%**
Estimated population misstatement rate = (round to nearest one-hundredth of a percent)	**0.06%**	*0*
Sample size (from table) =	**75**	**60**

Sample size = **75**
(choose larger of
the two above)

Oceanview Marine Company
Sample Selection: Monetary-Unit Sampling
December 31, 2007

Audit Area: *Accounts receivable*

Sampling Interval = Book value of population / Sample size = **22,000**

(round **down** to hundreds)

Random Starting Point = *8,000*

	Dollar unit	Physical Unit (Customer Name)	Amount Confirmed
1	*8,000*	*James Abbott*	*21,345.00*
2	**30,000**	**Anthony Underwriters**	**117,990.00**
3	**52,000**	**Anthony Underwriters**	**117,990.00**
4	**74,000**	**Anthony Underwriters**	**117,990.00**
5	**96,000**	**Anthony Underwriters**	**117,990.00**
6	**118,000**	**Anthony Underwriters**	**117,990.00**
7	**140,000**	**Anthony Underwriters**	**117,990.00**
8	**162,000**	**Lonnie Beatty**	**21,390.00**
9	**184,000**	**John Bischoff**	**113,655.00**
10	*206,000*	*John Bischoff*	*113,655.00*
11 to 80	*Various*	*Various*	

Oceanview Marine Company
Evaluation of A/R Confirmations: Monetary-Unit Sampling
December 31, 2007

Summary of Confirmation Differences:

Customer Name	A/R Balance per Client's Records	A/R Balance per Customer	Amount of Difference	Reason(s) for Difference	Amount of client misstatement, if any Over (Under)	Unit Misstatement (misstatement/ AR balance per client's records) Over (Under)
Robert Borst	155,690.00	0.00	155,690.00	Timing difference; not an exception.	0.00	N/A
Richard Howard	11,678.00	11,561.00	117.00	Client failed to issue credit memo.	117.00	0.0101
Diane Meier	21,456.90	19,256.90	2,200.00	Pricing error on floor model.	2,200.00	0.1026
Paul Steinbart	13,654.00	16,354.00	-2,700.00	Transposition error.	-2,700.00	-0.1978
John Underwood	46,770.00	47,660.00	-890.00	Transposition error.	-890.00	-0.0191

Net Misstatement: **-1,273.00**

Percent Misstatement Bounds:

Number of misstatements	Upper precision limit (from Table 2 in appendix)	Increase in precision limit resulting from each misstatement ("layers")
0	0.0156	0.0156
1	0.0292	0.0136
2	0.0423	0.0131
3	0.0548	0.0125
4	0.0670	0.0122

Calculation of Initial Overstatement Bound:

Number of overstatements	Upper precision limit portion	Recorded population value	Unit misstatement assumption (100% for zero misstatements)	Misstatement bound portion (Columns 2 x 3 x 4)
0	0.0156	1,762,682.00	1.0000	**27,497.84**
1	0.0136	1,762,682.00	**0.1026**	**2,459.58**
2	0.0131	1,762,682.00	**0.0101**	**233.22**
3	0.0125	1,762,682.00		
4	0.0122	1,762,682.00		
			Initial overstatement bound =	**30,190.64**

Calculation of Initial Understatement Bound:

Number of understatements	Lower precision limit portion	Recorded population value	Unit misstatement assumption (100% for zero misstatements)	Misstatement bound portion (Columns 2 x 3 x 4)
0	0.0156	1,762,682.00	1.0000	**27,497.84**
1	0.0136	1,762,682.00	**0.1978**	**4,741.76**
2	0.0131	1,762,682.00	**0.0191**	**441.04**
3	0.0125	1,762,682.00		
4	0.0122	1,762,682.00		
			Initial understatement bound =	**32,680.64**

Calculation of Point Estimate for Overstatements:

Number of overstatements	Unit misstatement assumption	Sample size	Recorded population	Columns 2 x 4 / 3 (round to 2 decimals)
1	**0.1026**	80	1,762,682.00	**2,260.64**
2	**0.0101**	80	1,762,682.00	**222.54**
3		80	1,762,682.00	
4		80	1,762,682.00	

Overstatement point estimate = **2,483.18**

Calculation of Point Estimate for Understatements:

Number of understatements	Unit misstatement assumption	Sample size	Recorded population	Columns 2 x 4 / 3 (round to 2 decimals)
1	**0.1978**	80	1,762,682.00	**4,358.23**
2	**0.0191**	80	1,762,682.00	**420.84**
3		80	1,762,682.00	
4		80	1,762,682.00	

Understatement point estimate = **4,779.07**

Calculation of Adjusted Misstatement Bounds:

Initial overstatement bound =	**30,190.64**
Less: Understatement point estimate =	**4,779.07**
Adjusted overstatement bound =	**25,411.57**
Initial understatement bound =	**32,680.64**
Less: Overstatement point estimate =	**2,483.18**
Adjusted understatement bound =	**30,197.46**

Decision (check one):

☐ Accept population as stated.
(No adjustment required for account to be fairly stated.)

☑ Request client adjust population.
(Account is not fairly stated, but if client corrects misstatements found in sample, account will be acceptable.)

☐ Expand audit tests.
(Account is not fairly stated, and cannot be made acceptable by correcting misstatements found in sample.)

☐ Some other action. Specify:

Explain/Justify your Decision:

The account balance is materially understated — the understatement bound (30,197) exceeds tolerable misstatement for understatements (30,000). If the client corrects the actual misstatements found in accounts receivable, the account balance would increase by $1,273. Accounts receivable would then be acceptable, as the upper and lower bounds would become $26,685 and 28,924, respectively.

(**Note to instructor:** Some students may check the first box, reasoning that an understatement of accounts receivable is not a significant concern. Some students may also recommend a larger adjustment or more testing, reasoning that the adjusted bounds are still close to tolerable misstatement.)

Conclusion:

Accounts receivable balance is materially misstated. In our opinion, however, the balance will be fairly stated after the client corrects all misstatements found during testing. No additional testing deemed necessary.

Calculation of Unadjusted Projected Misstatement:

Overstatement point estimate	**2,483.18**	
less: Understatement point estimate	**4,779.07**	
equals: **Projected misstatement**	**-2,295.89**	**(understated)**
less: Adjusting journal entry *(21-2)*	**1,273.00**	**(increase)**
equals: **Unadjusted projected misstatement**	**-1,022.89**	**(understated)**

carry forward to *Summary of Possible Misstatements* (workpaper 90-1)

Oceanview Marine Company
Calculation of Sample Size: Monetary-Unit Sampling
December 31, 2007

Audit Area: *Accounts receivable*

Population: *Book value of accounts receivable $1,762,682*

Sampling Unit: *Dollars in accounts receivable at 12/31/07*

Decision and Facts for Determining Sample Size:

Book value of population = *1,762,682*

Acceptable risk of incorrect acceptance = **30%**

Tolerable misstatement = **30,000**

Estimated misstatement in the population = *1,000* *(overstated)*

Reliability factor (from table below) = **1.20**

Expansion factor (from table below) = **1.20**

ARIA	Reliability Factors	Expansion Factors
5%	3.00	1.60
10%	2.30	1.50
20%	1.61	1.30
30%	1.20	1.20
50%	0.69	1.10

Calculation of Sample Size:

	Upper Bound	Lower Bound
(a) Book value of population =	1,762,682	1,762,682
(b) Reliability factor =	1.20	1.20
(a) * (b) = Numerator	2,115,218.40	2,115,218.40
(c) Tolerable misstatement =	30,000	30,000
(d) Estimated misstatement =	1,000	0
(e) Expansion factor =	1.20	1.20
(c) - (d*e) = Denominator	28,800.00	30,000.00
Sample size =	73.45	70.51

Sample size = **74**

(choose larger of the two above)

(round **up** to whole number)

Oceanview Marine Company
Sample Selection: Monetary-Unit Sampling
December 31, 2007

Audit Area: *Accounts receivable*

Sampling Interval = Book value of population / Sample size = **22,000**

(round **down** to hundreds)

Random Starting Point = *8,000*

	Dollar unit	Physical Unit (Customer Name)	Amount Confirmed
1	*8,000*	*James Abbott*	*21,345.00*
2	**30,000**	**Anthony Underwriters**	**117,990.00**
3	**52,000**	**Anthony Underwriters**	**117,990.00**
4	**74,000**	**Anthony Underwriters**	**117,990.00**
5	**96,000**	**Anthony Underwriters**	**117,990.00**
6	**118,000**	**Anthony Underwriters**	**117,990.00**
7	**140,000**	**Anthony Underwriters**	**117,990.00**
8	**162,000**	**Lonnie Beatty**	**21,390.00**
9	**184,000**	**John Bischoff**	**113,655.00**
10	*206,000*	*John Bischoff*	*113,655.00*
11 to 80	*Various*	*Various*	

Oceanview Marine Company
Evaluation of A/R Confirmations: Monetary-Unit Sampling
December 31, 2007

Summary of Confirmation Differences:

Customer Name	A/R Balance per Client's Records	A/R Balance per Customer	Amount of Difference	Reason(s) for Difference	Amount of client misstatement, if any Over (Under)	Tainting (misstatement/ AR balance per client's records) Over (Under)
Robert Borst	155,690.00	0.00	155,690.00	Timing difference; not an exception.	0.00	N/A
Richard Howard	11,678.00	11,561.00	117.00	Client failed to issue credit memo.	117.00	0.0101
Diane Meier	21,456.90	19,256.90	2,200.00	Pricing error on floor model.	2,200.00	0.1026
Paul Steinbart	13,654.00	16,354.00	-2,700.00	Transposition error.	-2,700.00	-0.1978
John Underwood	46,770.00	47,660.00	-890.00	Transposition error.	-890.00	-0.0191

Net Misstatement: **-1,273.00**

Calculation of Projected Misstatement:

Customer Name	Tainting	Sampling Interval	Projected Misstatement
Richard Howard	.0101	22,000	222.20
Diane Meier	.1026	22,000	2,257.20
Paul Steinbart	-.1978	22,000	-4,351.60
John Underwood	N/A	N/A	-890.00

Net Projected Misstatement = **-2,762.20**

Evaluation of A/R Confirmations: Monetary-Unit Sampling
December 31, 2007

Calculation of Basic Precision:

Sampling Interval	x	Reliability Factor	=	Basic Precision
22,000		**1.20**		**26,400.00**

Calculation of Incremental Allowance for Overstatements:

Projected Misstatements	x	Incremental Increase in Reliability Factors (minus 1)	=	Incremental Allowance
2,257.20		0.24		**541.73**
222.20		0.18		**40.00**
		0.14		
		0.13		
		0.12		

Incremental Allowance for Overstatements = **581.73**

Calculation of Incremental Allowance for Understatements:

Projected Misstatements	x	Incremental Increase in Reliability Factors (minus 1)	=	Incremental Allowance
4,351.60		0.24		**1,044.38**
		0.18		
		0.14		
		0.13		
		0.12		

Incremental Allowance for Understatements = **1,044.38**

Calculation of Upper and Lower Misstatement Limits:

Net Projected Misstatement =	**-2,762.20**
Add: Basic Precision =	**26,400.00**
Add: Incremental Allowance for Overstatements =	**581.73**
Upper Misstatement Limit =	**24,219.53**

Net Projected Misstatement =	**-2,762.20**
Less: Basic Precision =	**26,400.00**
Less: Incremental Allowance for Understatements =	**1,044.38**
Lower Misstatement Limit =	**-30,206.58**

Decision (check one):

☐   Accept population as stated.
(No adjustment required for account to be fairly stated.)

☑   Request client adjust population.
(Account is not fairly stated, but if client corrects misstatements found in sample, account will be acceptable.)

☐   Expand audit tests.
(Account is not fairly stated, and cannot be made acceptable by correcting misstatements found in sample.)

☐   Some other action. Specify:

Explain/Justify your Decision:

The account balance is materially understated — the understatement bound (30,207) exceeds tolerable misstatement for understatements (30,000). If the client corrects the actual misstatements found in accounts receivable, the account balance would increase by $1,273. Accounts receivable would then be acceptable, as the upper and lower bounds would become $25,493 and 28,934, respectively.

(**Note to instructor:** Some students may check the first box, reasoning that an understatement of accounts receivable is not a significant concern. Some students may also recommend a larger adjustment or more testing, reasoning that the adjusted bounds are still close to tolerable misstatement.)

Conclusion:

Accounts receivable balance is materially misstated. In our opinion, however, the balance will be fairly stated after the client corrects all misstatements found during testing. No additional testing deemed necessary

Calculation of Unadjusted Projected Misstatement:

Net projected misstatement __**-2,762.20**__ **(understated)**

less: Adjusting journal entry *(21-2)* __**1,273.00**__ **(increase)**

equals: **Unadjusted projected misstatement** __**-1,489.20**__ **(understated)**
carry forward to *Summary of Possible Misstatements* (workpaper 90-1)

XX 2/24/08

Oceanview Marine Company
Calculation of Sample Size: Difference Estimation
December 31, 2007

Audit Area: *Accounts receivable*
Population: *86 accounts receivable at 12/31/07*

Decision and Facts for Determining Sample Size:

Population (number of accounts) (N) =	*86*
Tolerable misstatement (TM) =	**30,000**
Estimated misstatement in the population (E) =	*1,000* (overstated)
Estimated population standard deviation (SD) =	*1,800*
Z_A (from table below) =	**0.52**
Z_R (from table below) =	**0.52**

Calculation of Sample Size:

$SD\,(Z_A + Z_R)\,N =$	**160,992.00**
$TM - E =$	**29,000.00**
$(SD\,(Z_A + Z_R)\,N)\,/\,(TM - E) =$	**5.55**
$[(SD\,(Z_A + Z_R)\,N)\,/\,(TM - E)]^2 =$	**30.82**
Sample Size =	**31**

(round **up** to whole number)

Acceptable Risk of Incorrect Acceptance (ARIA) (check one):

(ARIA should be based on considerations of acceptable audit risk, inherent risk, control risk, results of preliminary analytical procedures, and the results of any relevant substantive tests of transactions already performed.)

		ARIA	Z_A(Conf. Coef.)
☐	Low (high amount of assurance needed from tests)	10	1.28
☑	Medium	30	0.52
☐	High (low amount of assurance needed from tests)	50	0.00

Acceptable Risk of Incorrect Rejection (ARIR) (check one):

(ARIR should be based on the costs of increasing the preliminary sample size and normally should be set at high unless there are unusual factors that affect the cost of increasing the sample size.)

		ARIR	Z_R(Conf. Coef.)
☐	Low	20	1.28
☐	Medium	40	0.84
☑	High	60	0.52

Oceanview Marine Company
Sample Selection: Difference Estimation
December 31, 2007

Audit Area: *Accounts receivable*

Sampling Interval = Number of accounts / Sample Size = _____ **2** _____

(round **down** to whole number)

Random Starting Point = *1st account*

	Customer Name	Amount Confirmed
1	*James Abbott*	*21,345.00*
2	**Robert Allen**	**432.00**
3	**Anthony Underwriters**	**117,990.00**
4	**Lonnie Beatty**	**21,390.00**
5	**Alex Binkowski**	**1,349.02**
6	**Robert Borst**	**155,690.00**
7	**Daniel Chappelle**	**24,678.00**
8	**Stephen Coscarelli**	**145.56**
9	**Richard Detzler**	**1,145.00**
10	*Amitabh Dugar*	*369.33*
11 to 35	*Various*	*Various*

Oceanview Marine Company
Evaluation of A/R Confirmations: Difference Estimation
December 31, 2007

Summary of Confirmation Differences:

Customer Name	A/R Balance per Client's Records	A/R Balance per Customer	Amount of Difference	Reason(s) for Difference	Amount of client misstatement, if any Over (Under)	Squared Misstatement
Robert Borst	155,690.00	0.00	155,690.00	Timing difference; not an exception.	0.00	N/A
Richard Howard	11,678.00	11,561.00	117.00	Client failed to issue credit memo.	117.00	13,689
Diane Meier	21,456.90	19,256.90	2,200.00	Pricing error on floor model.	2,200.00	4,840,000
Paul Steinbart	13,654.00	16,354.00	-2,700.00	Transposition error.	-2,700.00	7,290,000
John Underwood	46,770.00	47,660.00	-890.00	Transposition error.	-890.00	792,100
Totals:					**-1,273.00**	**12,935,789**

Calculation of Projected Misstatement:

Total amount of misstatement in sample per table above =	**-1,273.00**
Sample size (# of accounts tested) =	**35**
Mean misstatement (total misstatements/sample size) =	**-36.37**
Population size (total # of accounts) =	**86**
Projected Misstatement (mean misstatement x population size) =	**-3,128** (understated)

Oceanview Marine Company
Evaluation of A/R Confirmations: Difference Estimation (continued)
December 31, 2007

Calculation of Sample Standard Deviation: (round all figures to whole numbers)

(a) Sum of squared misstatements in the sample = **12,935,789**

Mean misstatement squared = **1,323**

(b) Mean misstatement squared x sample size = **46,305**

(a) - (b) = **12,889,484**

(c) [(a) - (b)] / (sample size - 1) = **379,102**

Square root of (c) = **616**

Sample Standard Deviation = **616**

Calculation of Precision Interval:

Population size (N) = *86*

Z_A (per 21-35) = **0.52** (round to 2 decimals)

(a) N x Z_A = **44.72** (round to 2 decimals)

Sample standard deviation (SD) (per above) = **616**

Square root of sample size = **5.92** (round to 2 decimals)

(b) SD / Square root of sample size = **104.05** (round to 2 decimals)

Population size (N) - sample size (n) = *51*

[(N) - (n)] / (N) = **0.59** (round to 2 decimals)

(c) Square root of [(N) - (n) / (N)] = **0.77** (round to 2 decimals)

Precision Interval (a x b x c) = **3,583**

(round to whole number)

Calculation of Confidence Limits:

Projected Misstatement (per 21-37) = **-3,128** (understated)

Add: Precision Interval (per 21-38) = **3,583**

Upper Confidence Limit = **455** (overstated)

Projected Misstatement (per 21-37) = **-3,128** (understated)

Less: Precision Interval (per 21-38) = **3,583**

Lower Confidence Limit = **-6,711** (understated)

Decision (check one):

☑ Accept population as stated.
(No adjustment required for account to be fairly stated.)

☐ Request client adjust population.
(Account is not fairly stated, but if client corrects misstatements found in sample, account will be acceptable.)

☐ Expand audit tests.
(Account is not fairly stated, and cannot be made acceptable by correcting misstatements found in sample.)

☐ Some other action. Specify:

Explain/Justify your Decision:

Both the upper and lower confidence limits are less than the tolerable misstatement for over- and understatements ($30,000). Accordingly, accounts receivable is deemed fairly stated.

Conclusion:

Based on the results of our tests, accounts receivable is considered fairly stated. No additional testing deemed necessary.

Calculation of Unadjusted Projected Misstatement:

Net projected misstatement **-3,128** (understated)

less: Adjusting journal entry *(21-2)* **1,273** (increase)

equals: **Unadjusted projected misstatement** **-1,855** (understated)
carry forward to *Summary of Possible Misstatements* (workpaper 90-1)

Oceanview Marine Company
Inventories Leadsheet
December 31, 2007

Account Number and Name	2007 Balance	Net Adjustments	2007 Adjusted Balance	2006 Balance	% Change (before adjustment)
2205 — Inventory, Boats	13,167,170 G/L	**27,851** **30-2***	**13,195,021**	12,030,247 PY	9.45%
2210 — Inventory, Repair Parts	200,390 G/L	**0**	**200,390**	182,983 PY	9.51%
2215 — Inventory, Supplies	156,789 G/L	**0**	**156,789**	143,170 PY	9.51%
Total	13,524,349 F 22-10		**13,552,200**	12,356,400 F	9.45%

Tickmark legend

G/L   _Agreed to general ledger._

PY   _Agreed to prior year's workpapers._

F   _Footed without exception._

*   **Note to instructor**: The adjustment to account 1205—Inventory, Boats comes from the audit of Account Payable; see workpaper 30-2.

AUDIT PROCEDURES	*	W/P	INIT	COMMENTS
29. Select items of inventory and: (a) review and note current selling prices and quantities sold,	A		BC	*Done for same sample as test counts. In each case the selling price is significantly higher than cost.*
(b) compare the inventory carrying amounts and recent selling prices for the selected items and ascertain that the carrying amounts are not in excess of net realizable value,	Rv		BC	*Noted two boats sold early in Jan. (#8062 and #8316). Both sold for more than cost.*
(c) compare quantities on hand for selected items with quantities noted per recent sales invoices and customer orders to determine if inventories appear reasonable in relation to requirements.	A	2-1	BC	*Inventory turnover ratios have been consistent for several years. Sales volume is up slightly, so slight increase in inventory is reasonable.*
30. Inquire of employees and management concerning obsolete inventory, and be alert for items that are damaged, rust- or dust-covered, or located in inappropriate places.	Rv	22-11	BC	*Discussed with Arvin Phillips. List of obsolete inventory prepared. Includes damaged, outdated, and unrepairable items.*
31. Obtain the client's Final Inventory Listing and verify additions and extensions on the listing.	D	22-8 to 22-10	BC	*No exceptions found.*
32. Trace from: (a) inventory count sheets to final inventory listing, and,	A Co	**22-8 to 22-10;** 22-12	**XX**	
(b) final inventory listing to inventory count sheets.	A E	to **22-14**	**XX**	
33. Select a sample of inventory items on the Final Inventory Listing and compare the inventory prices with prices per recent vendors' invoices, price lists, or published quotations.	A	22-16 22-17 **22-18** to **22-20**	**XX**	
Other procedures: *Compare client final listing to count sheets.*	A	22-8 to 22-10 22-12	BC	
For cutoff information obtained at year end, check that goods received on or before the cutoff date have been included in inventory, goods shipped on or before the cutoff date have been excluded from inventory, goods received after the cutoff date have been excluded from inventory, and goods shipped after the cutoff date have been included in inventory.	Cu	to 22-14	BC	*In separate file.*

* **Audit Objectives:**
Accuracy   Classification   Completeness   Cutoff   Detail tie-in   Existence
Presentation and disclosure   Realizable value   Rights and obligations

AUDIT PROCEDURES	*	W/P	INIT	COMMENTS

ANALYTICAL PROCEDURES

AUDIT PROCEDURES	*	W/P	INIT	COMMENTS
34. Test the reasonableness of inventory by: (a) comparison with prior years, (b) application of the gross margin percentage method, (c) computing the rate of turnover, (d) reference to capacity of storage facilities.	E Co A	2-1	BC	*Year-end balance is up by 9.5%, but sales are up by 15.6%* *No significant variance from prior years.* *No unusual variance.*
35. Compare gross profit percentage, by product line if possible, of current year to prior year; obtain explanations for significant variances.	E Co A		BC	*Variance negligible.*
Other procedures:			BC	*None*

STATEMENT PRESENTATION

AUDIT PROCEDURES	*	W/P	INIT	COMMENTS
36. Verify basis of inventory valuation is clearly stated.	P		BC	
37. Verify that any changes in the basis of valuation are stated.	P		BC	*No changes*
Other procedures:			BC	*None*

CONCLUSION

38. State, in your opinion, if the inventory reported in the financial statements is fairly presented and is in accordance with GAAP.

In our opinion, inventory is fairly stated in accordance with GAAP.

* **Audit Objectives:**
   Accuracy   Classification   Completeness   Cutoff   Detail tie-in   **Existence**
   Presentation and disclosure   Realizable value   Rights and obligations

From count sheets:　　　　*8111*　　*Results/discrepancies noted:*

*Select every tenth
item from the count
sheets (w/p 22-12 to
22-14), starting with
stock #8111 and
agree to final listings.*

8550
8124
8243
8257
8113
8524
8428
8800
8679

No exceptions found.

From final listings:　　　*8009*　　*Results/discrepancies noted:*

*Select every tenth
item from final
listings (w/p 22-8 to
22-10), starting with
stock #8009 and
agree to the count
sheets.*

8123
8245
8259
8365
8428
8503
8548
8668
8778

No exceptions found.

Results of Inventory Pricing Tests: Non-statistical
As at December 31, 2007

Summary of Misstatements:

Boat Stock Number	Recorded Inventory Amount	Amount per Vendor's Invoice	Amount of Difference	Reason(s) for Difference	Amount of Client Misstatement, if any Over (under)
8114	109,995.00	112,495.00	-2,500.00	Freight not included.	-2,500.00
8444	44,565.00	45,465.00	-900.00	Transposition error.	-900.00
8775	40,665.00	38,005.00	2,660.00	Client recorded boat as a Camano Troll, rather than Campion Troll.	2,660.00

Net misstatement in sample = **-740.00**

90-1

Calculation of Projected Misstatement:

Net misstatement in sample x Population size (in $) / Sample size (in $) = **-2,273.00**

90-1

Calculation of Allowance for Sampling Error:

Tolerable misstatement = *50,000*

less: Projected misstatement = **2,273**

Allowance for sampling error = **47,727**

Decision (check one):

☑ Accept population as stated.
(No adjustment required for account to be fairly stated.)

☐ Request client adjust population.
(Account is not fairly stated, but if client corrects misstatements found in sample, account will be acceptable.)

☐ Expand audit tests.
(Account is not fairly stated, and cannot be made acceptable by correcting misstatements found in sample.)

☐ Some other action. Specify:

Explain/Justify your Decision:

Allowance for sampling error is sufficiently large to conclude that inventory is fairly stated.

Conclusion:

Based on the results of our tests, inventory appears to be fairly stated. No additional testing deemed necessary.

Oceanview Marine Company
Accounts Payable Leadsheet
December 31, 2007

Account Number and Name	2007 Balance	Net Adjustments		2007 Adjusted Balance	2006 Balance	% Change (before adjustment)
2010 — Accounts payable *30-10*	1,750,831 *G/L*	**30-2**	**30,101**	**1,780,932**	1,403,247 *PY*	24.77%

Tickmark legend

G/L   *Agreed to general ledger.*

PY   *Agreed to prior year's workpapers.*

Account Number and Name	Debit	Credit
6020 Advertising expense	**2,250**	
2010 Accounts payable – Salt, Sand & Sea Adv.		**2,250**
		30-1
Explanation: AJE for unrecorded liability at year-end		
1205 Inventory – Boats	**27,851.15**	
2010 Accounts payable – Anderson Marine	**22-1**	**27,851.15**
		30-1
Explanation: AJE for unrecorded liability at year-end		

AUDIT PROCEDURES

	*	INIT	W/P	COMMENTS
4. Obtain list of cash disbursements after year-end to perform search for unrecorded liabilities and tests of year-end payables balances:	A Co Ro	*BC*	*30-11 to 30-19*	
a. determine sample size for testing;		*BC*	*30-20*	
b. select sample items for testing;		**XX**	**30-21**	**Sample per 30-21.**
c. trace amounts representing accounts payable at year-end to listing of accounts payable;		**XX**	**to 30-23**	
d. evaluate and summarize any payments representing potential omissions or misstatements of year-end accounts;		**XX**		
e. generalize misstatements to population and evaluate acceptability of the population.		**XX**		

ANALYTICAL PROCEDURES

	*	INIT	W/P	COMMENTS
5. Compare accounts payable and accrued liabilities in the current year to prior years and obtain explanations for significant differences.	E Co A	*BC*		*Increase due to higher volume and increased inventory.*

STATEMENT PRESENTATION

	*	INIT	W/P	COMMENTS
6. Determine if groupings are consistent with previous periods.	P	*BC*		*Yes. Consistent.*
7. Reclassify any debit balances.	A P	*BC*		*None*
8. Verify that accounts payable is classified as a current liability on the balance sheet.	P	*BC*		*Done*

* **Audit Objectives:**
Accuracy   Classification   Completeness   Cutoff   Detail tie-in   Existence
Presentation and disclosure   Rights and obligations

AUDIT PROCEDURES

CONCLUSION

9. State, in your opinion, if the accounts payable balance reported in the financial statements is fairly presented and is in accordance with GAAP.

> **In our opinion, accounts payable is fairly stated in accordance with GAAP.**

Oceanview Marine Company
Sample Selection: Non-statistical Sampling — A/P
December 31, 2007

Audit Area: *Accounts payable - Tests of subsequent cash disbursements*

Describe Sample Selection Method:

Stratum 1:All cash disbursements greater than tolerable misstatement of $30,000.

Stratum 2:Sample of all remaining cash disbursements (≤ $30,000)

Sampling Interval = Number of Cash Disbursements / Sample Size =　　　**8**

Random Starting Point: 3rd check issued in Jan 08

(round **down** to whole number)

Stratum 1:

	Check #	Customer Name	Amount Tested
1	6278	*Luxury Boats*	*41,034.56*
2	**6293**	**Tradewind Marine**	**60,122.93**
3	**6308**	**Luxury Boats**	**55,863.89**
4	**6324**	**Great Outdoor Boats**	**95,236.90**
5	6330	*Nordic Powerboats*	*162,412.65*
6 to 20	*Various*	*Various*	*662,918.17*

Population size (in dollars) of stratum 1　**1,077,589.10**

Stratum 2:

	Check #	Customer Name	Amount Tested
1	6272	*Breeze Sailboats*	*23,476.09*
2	**6281**	**Anderson Marine**	**3,218.17**
3	**6289**	**Salt, Sand & Sea Advertising**	**2,250.00**
4	**6298**	**Anderson Marine**	**27,851.15**
5	6306	*Kip's Engine Specialties*	*56.34*
6 to 15	*Various*	*Various*	*77,700.84*

Sample size (in dollars) of stratum 2　**134,552.59**

Evaluation of Tests of Subsequent Disbursements — Non-statistical

30-22
XX 2/25/08

December 31, 2007

Summary of Misstatements:

Vendor Name	A/P Balance per Client's Records	Correct A/P Balance	Amount of Misstatement Over (Under)	Nature of Misstatement
Salt, Sand, & Sea Adv.	0.00	2,250.00	**-2,250.00**	**Understatement of accounts payable**
Anderson Marine	0.00	27,851.15	**-27,851.15**	**Understatement of accounts payable**

Net Misstatement: **-30,101.15**

Calculation of Projected Misstatement:

Net misstatement x population size (in dollars) / sample size (in dollars) =   **-50,427.43**

Calculation of Allowance for Sampling Error:

Tolerable misstatement =	**30,000.00**
Less: Projected misstatement =	**50,427.43**
Allowance for Sampling Error =	**None**

Oceanview Marine Company
Evaluation of Tests of Subsequent Disbursements—Non-statistical (Continued)
December 31, 2007

30-23
XX 2/25/08

Decision (check one):

☐ Accept population as stated.
(No adjustment required for account to be fairly stated.)

☑ Request client adjust population.
(Account is not fairly stated, but if client corrects misstatements found in sample, account will be acceptable.)

☐ Expand audit tests.
(Account is not fairly stated, and cannot be made acceptable by correcting misstatements found in sample.)

☐ Some other action. Specify:

Explain/Justify your Decision:

The account balance is materially understated. However, once the client corrects the misstatements found, the account will be acceptable.

Conclusion:

Accounts payable balance is materially understated. In our opinion, however, the balance will be fairly stated after the client corrects the actual misstatements found during testing. No additional testing deemed necessary.

Calculation of Unadjusted Projected Misstatement:

Net projected misstatement __**-50,427.43**__ (understated)

less: Adjusting journal entry (net) __**30,101.15**__ (increase)

Unadjusted projected misstatement __**-20,326.28**__ (understated)
carry forward to *Summary of Possible Misstatements* (workpaper 90-1)

Oceanview Marine Company
Summary of Possible Misstatements
December 31, 2007

Description of Misstatement	W/P Reference	Identified Misstatement	Likely Aggregate Misstatement	Possible Misstatements – Overstatement (Understatement)			
				Current Assets	Noncurrent Assets	Current Liabilities	Income Before Taxes
Obsolete inventory	22-11	10,900	10,900	10,900			10,900
Understated prepaid insurance	23-2	(4,350)	(4,350)	(4,350)			(4,350)
Understated accrued bonuses	31-2	(2,987)	(2,987)			(2,987)	2,987
Accounts receivable:							
Option A – Understatement	21-21	0	(303)	(303)			(303)
Option B – Understatement	21-28	0	(1,023)	(1,023)			(1,023)
Option C – Understatement	21-34	0	(1,489)	(1,489)			(1,489)
Option D – Understatement	21-40	0	(1,855)	(1,855)			(1,855)
Understated accounts payable	30-23	0	(20,326)			(20,326)	20,326
Understated inventory	22-18	(740)	(2,273)	(2,273)			(2,273)
a. Totals							
Option A completed in Assignment 6				3,974	0	(23,313)	27,287
Option B completed in Assignment 6				3,254	0	(23,313)	26,567
Option C completed in Assignment 6				2,788	0	(23,313)	26,101
Option D completed in Assignment 6				2,422	0	(23,313)	25,735
b. Adjusted measurement base (e.g., adjusted net income before taxes)				936,772	936,772	936,772	936,772
c. Materiality % applied to base				7.50%	7.50%	7.50%	7.50%
d. Materiality (b x c) (rounded)				70,000	70,000	70,000	70,000
e. Amount remaining for further possible misstatements (d - |a|)							
Option A completed in Assignment 6				66,026	70,000	46,687	42,713
Option B completed in Assignment 6				66,746	70,000	46,687	43,433
Option C completed in Assignment 6				67,212	70,000	46,687	43,889
Option D completed in Assignment 6				67,578	70,000	46,687	44,265

Conclusion: Amounts remaining for further possible misstatements appear adequate.

Suggested solutions

1. *The company pays significant amounts of dividends because of the passive ownership interest of Southeastern Enterprises. These dividends are not deductible for income tax purposes. Purchasing the stock of these outside investors, by borrowing against equity, could eliminate the need for dividends. Alternatively, the company could consider becoming an S Corporation. However, this option should be carefully evaluated in light of the company's plans to go public in the future.*

2. *During our tests of internal controls over sales transactions, we noted that, on occasion, merchandise is shipped to customers without prior credit approval. We recommend that steps be taken to ensure that all shipments are supported by approved customer orders and authorized shipping documents, and that all such approvals be made prior to shipment. In addition, we recommend that management implement an internal verification policy to check for proper debit/credit classification for sales transactions.*

3. *During our observation of the physical inventory count taken by your employees, we noted that approximately $11,000 of obsolete inventory was included in the count. We recommend that on an annual basis, all obsolete inventory be physically segregated from the rest of the inventory prior to the year-end count and that procedures be implemented to remove obsolete inventory from the general ledger.*

4. *During our observation of the physical inventory count, we also noted that the parts storeroom did not appear to be adequately secured. Several of the storage areas were disorganized, and the storeroom did not have locks on all entrances. We recommend that you install proper locks on all entrances and that each storage area be better organized to increase the likelihood of an accurate count and decrease the risk of loss.*

5. **Management may want to consider taking on more debt to buy out Southeastern Enterprises.**
(from Assignment 2)

   (Note to instructor: Some students might recommend that Oceanview work toward reducing their level of debt, stating that the liabilities to owners' equity ratios have been increasing. However, relative to the industry averages, the liabilities to owners' equity ratios are relatively low.)

6. **Management may want to consider tightening its credit policies.** (from Assignment 2)

   (**Note to instructor:** While many of your students will probably make this recommendation, you may want to point out that management believes the current credit policy is a major factor in Oceanview's success.)

   (Additional acceptable responses for Assignment 2 will vary from student to student)

7. **Employees should be reminded of the importance of proper approval of acquisitions prior to mailing purchase orders to vendors.** (from Assignment 5)

8. **Management should implement an internal control policy that encourages the timely recording of acquisitions.** (from Assignment 5)

9. **Additional recommendation** (from Assignment 10)

   (**Note to instructor:** In Assignment 10, students are required to add one more recommendation to this letter, based on their work in Assignments 1 through 10. Acceptable responses will, of course, vary from student to student.)

Independent Auditor's Report

To: The Shareholders of Oceanview Marine Company

We have audited the accompanying balance sheet of Oceanview Marine Company as of December 31, 2007, and the related statements of income, retained earnings, and cash flows for the year then ended. These financial statements are the responsibility of Oceanview Marine Company's management. Our responsibility is to express an opinion on these financial statements based on our audit. The financial statements of Oceanview Marine Company as of December 31, 2006 and 2005 were audited by other auditors whose reports dated March 29, 2007 and March 15, 2006 expressed an unqualified opinion on those statements.

We conducted our audit in accordance with auditing standards generally accepted in the United States of America. Those standards require that we plan and perform the audit to obtain reasonable assurance about whether the financial statements are free of material misstatement. An audit includes examining, on a test basis, evidence supporting the amounts and disclosures in the financial statements. An audit also includes assessing the accounting principles used and significant estimates made by management, as well as evaluating the overall financial statement presentation. We believe that our audit provides a reasonable basis for our opinion.

In our opinion, the financial statements referred to above present fairly, in all material respects, the financial position of Oceanview Marine Company as of December 31, 2007, and the results of its operations and its cash flows for the year then ended in conformity with accounting principles generally accepted in the United States of America.

February 26, 2008

Lilts Berger & Associates
Certified Public Accountants
Ocean City, Florida

Recommended answers to discussion questions _____

Assignment 1

1.

Factors Favoring Acceptance	Concerns About Acceptance
1. *Responses to inquiries to predecessor auditor were complimentary about Oceanview. Predecessor auditor spoke highly of Oceanview's employees' integrity, competence, and dedication to running a successful business.*	1. Oceanview is considering going public in the near future. Lilts Berger & Associates, CPAs, may or may not want to be involved in taking a client public.
2. Oceanview is a well-established, successful, non-public financially healthy business (low business risk for Lilts Berger & Associates, CPAs).	2. Oceanview's president, vice-president, and controller are all related which could increase the possibility of collusion against Southeastern Enterprises. This also increases the possibility of related-party transactions.
3. Reference checks with Oceanview's bank, attorney, and customers were favorable.	3. Oceanview has a very lenient credit policy, which may increase the possibility of future financial difficulties.

2. A CPA firm might charge a new client an audit fee that is less than the estimated first-year costs of performing the audit if the firm expects to make up the difference in future years. This could be done in a number of ways, including performing the audit more efficiently (and at lower cost) in future years, and by providing additional (and more profitable) services to the client, such as tax or consulting services.

3. a. The primary purpose of the communication between successor and predecessor auditors is to help the successor auditor decide whether to accept the engagement. If the potential client has a history of being difficult to work with, or has a history of questionable or unethical activities, or late or non-payments for professional services rendered in the past, the successor auditor may choose not to accept the engagement.

   b. Since rule 301 of the AICPA Code of Professional Conduct prohibits the auditors from disclosing confidential client information without the consent of the client, the client's permission is required before the predecessor auditor can respond to the successor auditor's request for information.

   c. The successor auditor typically reviews the predecessor auditor's working papers to help the successor auditor plan its first-time audit of the client. Prior years' working papers contain useful information about the client's business and industry, its accounting system and related internal controls, and about the nature and cause of misstatements discovered in the client's financial statement in prior years.

4. The basic nature of the engagement letter would not change if Oceanview were a publicly traded company. However, the nature and timing of the audit services to be provided would likely be affected, and the audit firm may provide additional services related to SEC filings. If Oceanview were a public company, the audit would be conducted under PCAOB auditing standards. The Sarbanes-Oxley Act and revised SEC rules on independence would also substantially restrict the ability of the firm to provide consulting services to Oceanview.

Recommended answers to discussion questions _____

Assignment 2

1. In the audit planning phase, the auditor uses *unaudited* account balances to perform *preliminary review* analytical procedures. The purposes of these preliminary analytical procedures are to (1) identify accounts that are more likely than others to contain material misstatements (often referred to as "attention-directing" analytical procedures), and (2) help the auditor assess the client's financial condition and ability to continue as a going concern. In addition, analytical procedures help the auditor understand the client's business and industry.

    In the *final review* stage, the auditor uses *audited* account balances to perform analytical procedures. The purposes of these analytical procedures are to (1) provide a final overview of the client's financial condition and reassess the going-concern assumption and (2) evaluate the overall reasonableness of the financial statement account balances and provide a final review for material misstatements in those accounts.

2. The auditor should assess the client's going concern status in the *planning* stage of the audit because the client's financial condition affects the nature, extent, and timing of audit procedures. The worse the client's financial condition, the lower the auditor's acceptable level of audit risk. In turn, the lower the acceptable level of audit risk, the greater the amount of assurance needed from the auditor's substantive procedures. Audit assurance can be increased by (1) increasing the extent of substantive testing, (2) performing more-reliable substantive procedures, or (3) performing substantive procedures closer to the balance sheet date.

3. Students' answers to this question will vary, as there is no "correct" answer. You may wish to discuss the fact that comparing current and prior years' balances as a percentage of sales has the advantage of compensating for variations in sales volume across years, and that variable expenses are expected to vary with sales while fixed expenses are not.

4. Any ratios or trends that indicate the client's financial condition is deteriorating or is poor would suggest an increased risk of fraud. Most students will probably answer that none of the fluctuations they identified represent an increased fraud risk, as Oceanview's financial condition is relatively strong.

Recommended answers to discussion questions _____

Assignment 3

1. The audit risk model specifies several factors that, along with planned detection risk and inherent risk, affect the extent of substantive testing:

   - the auditor's acceptable level of audit risk, which is influenced by the extent to which the financial statements will be relied on, the client's financial condition, and the client management's integrity;
   - control risk;
   - the results of preliminary analytical procedures.

   Additional factors that affect the extent of substantive testing include:
   - overall materiality level
   - tolerable misstatement (the allocation of materiality to each balance sheet account)

2. Acceptable audit risk, inherent risk, the preliminary judgment about materiality, and the allocation of materiality (tolerable misstatement) should be determined early in the audit because each of these factors influences the extent of substantive audit testing.

   Specifically, a greater extent of testing is necessary when *acceptable audit risk* is low, than when it is high; i.e., there is an inverse relationship between the level of acceptable audit risk and the extent of substantive testing. Similarly, there are inverse relationships between (1) the *preliminary materiality level* and the extent of testing, and (2) the amount of materiality (*tolerable misstatement*) allocated to a particular account and the extent of substantive testing to be performed on that account. Inherent risk is directly related to the extent of substantive tests; the higher an account's *inherent risk*, the greater the extent of testing of that account will be.

3. Since the levels of acceptable audit risk and materiality are both inversely related to the extent of substantive testing, lower levels of either one would result in an increase in the planned extent of substantive testing.

4. Oceanview's management has minimal incentives to engage in fraudulent financial reporting. The company is financially healthy and is not a publicly traded company. However, the company does have outside equity from Southeastern Enterprises. Family members hold key positions, and related parties exist, indicating opportunity for fraud. The somewhat adversarial relationship with Southeastern could provide a rationalization for financial transactions that benefit the majority family owners at the expense of the outside investors.

5. Students' answers to this question will vary. However, their answers should be consistent with the guidelines for setting tolerable misstatements found in the POLICY STATEMENT on page six in Assignment 3.

6. The sum of tolerable misstatements is allowed to exceed the preliminary judgment about materiality because (1) some accounts are likely to be overstated while other accounts are understated, resulting in a net misstatement that is likely to be less than the overall materiality level, and (2) it is unlikely that each account will be misstated by the full amount of its tolerable misstatement.

Assignment 4

1. The primary benefit of testing and relying on controls is a reduction in the extent of substantive testing. Since substantive testing is generally more costly than testing controls, this would reduce costs. Testing and relying on controls also allows the audit work to be spread more evenly across time—substantive tests are normally performed at or near year-end, whereas tests of controls can be performed prior to year end. Tests of controls also help the auditor assess the likelihood that monetary misstatements may have occurred in the client's accounting system during the period under audit.

2. The auditor would choose not to test controls whenever the anticipated costs of testing controls exceed the anticipated benefits. For instance, if the auditor's preliminary assessment of control risk for a particular objective or assertion is high (important control procedures related to that objective or assertion do not exist), the auditor would not spend time performing tests of controls related to that objective or assertion, since there would be no benefit (reduction in substantive testing) from such tests.

3. As the auditor's preliminary assessment of control risk decreases from the maximum, (a) the extent of tests of controls would increase, and (b) the extent of substantive tests of balances would decrease, assuming the tests of controls indicated the controls are reliable.

4. Flowcharts are useful for providing a clear and concise understanding of the client's accounting system and related internal controls. However, they can be fairly difficult to prepare. Internal control questionnaires are generally easier to complete than flowcharts, and once completed, clearly identify the client's control strengths and weaknesses in each accounting cycle (most control questionnaires are designed so that a "yes" response indicates a control strength while a "no" response indicates a control weakness). A weakness of standard, pre-printed questionnaires is that they may not be applicable to all clients. In addition, it is more difficult to obtain a clear overview of the client's accounting system from a questionnaire than from a flowchart.

5. A *significant deficiency* is a control, or combination of control deficiencies, that adversely affects the entity's ability to initiate, authorize, record, process, or report financial data reliably in accordance with generally accepted accounting principles such that there is more than a remote likelihood that a misstatement of the entity's financial statements that is more than inconsequential will not be prevented or detected. A *material weakness* is a significant deficiency, or combination of control deficiencies that results in more than a remote likelihood that a material misstatement of the financial statements will not be prevented or detected. Significant deficiencies and material weaknesses should be communicated in writing to management and those charged with governance.

None of the deficiencies in Oceanview's controls over acquisitions are serious enough to be considered significant deficiencies or material weaknesses.

Assignment 5

1. The *expected population exception rate* (EPER) is the auditor's advance estimate of the exception rate in the population. This estimate is normally based on the prior year's audit results. If prior results are not available, the auditor can test a small preliminary sample from the current year's population.

    The *tolerable exception rate* (TER) is based on the extent to which the auditor plans to rely on the control being tested (i.e., the importance of the control). If the auditor plans to place substantial reliance on the control, the tolerable exception rate should be between 2% and 7%. If little reliance is planned, the tolerable exception rate can be 10% or higher (*AICPA Audit Sampling Audit Practice Release*).

    The *acceptable risk of assessing control risk too low* (ARACR) depends primarily on the preliminary assessment of control risk. If control risk is assessed as low (i.e., the au tor plans to place substantial reliance on the control and reduce the extent of substantive tests of balances), then ARACR should be low. In most cases, ARACR should be set between 5% and 10%, inclusive.

2. When the computed upper exception rate (CUER) exceeds the tolerable exception rate (TER), the auditor will likely increase the assessed level of control risk and increase one or more related substantive tests. Other possible courses of action include:

    *   Increase the sample size. This will decrease the sampling error, causing the CUER to be nearer to the sample exception rate and, in some cases, less than the TER. However, increasing the sample size may also cause the sample exception rate to increase or decrease.

    *   Revise TER. If the auditor decides that the original TER was too conservative, he/she might choose to increase TER. However, this may be difficult to justify if called on to defend the decision in court.

    *   Write a letter to management. Regardless of which of the above courses of action is taken, whenever the auditor determines that internal controls are not operating effectively, the auditor should notify the client.

3. No, deficiencies in internal controls did not result in substantive misstatements in the recording of transactions. Deficiencies in internal control increase the *risk*, or *likelihood*, that significant misstatements will occur when recording transactions, but do not necessarily result in the actual occurrence of misstatements.

Recommended answers to discussion questions _____

Assignment 6

1. Confirmation of accounts receivable is not required when:

   - accounts receivable are immaterial, or

   - the auditor believes that confirmation will be ineffective because response rates are likely to be inadequate or unreliable, or

   - the combined level of inherent risk and control risk is low and other substantive procedures can be performed to achieve the audit objectives related to accounts receivable.

2. Risk of material misstatement related to revenue recognition indicates increased risk for the existence and cutoff objectives for accounts receivable. The auditor may address these risks by expanding the extent of confirmation testing, or through other procedures.

Assignment 7

1.   Confirmations are rarely used in the testing of accounts payable because external documentation usually exists to test the accounts payable balance. Confirmation may be appropriate when controls are ineffective, or if the auditor wishes to confirm the existence of specific terms or commitments related to purchases.

2.   The primary objective in the audit of accounts payable is to test the completeness of accounts payable. Because this involves testing for omitted amounts, it is much more difficult to define the population being tested compared to tests of the existence of recorded amounts. When testing for omitted payables, the auditor must still project errors to the population, but it is more common to use non-statistical sampling methods to evaluate the sample.

3.   Goods shipped FOB shipping point before year-end but received after year-end represent a liability as of the balance sheet date. Where material, the in-transit inventory and related liability should be recorded as of the balance sheet date. The auditor should examine documentation for material purchases received and recorded after year-end to determine if the goods were shipped FOB shipping point prior to year-end.

Recommended answers to discussion questions _____

Assignment 8

1. One possible explanation is that the checks were written shortly before the balance sheet date and have not had sufficient time to clear the bank. If this is the case, then there is no misstatement.

    Another possibility is that the cash disbursements journal was held open past year-end; i.e., the checks were written after the balance sheet date, but were recorded as if they were written prior to the balance sheet date. If this were the case, then the year-end cash balance would be understated.

2. This situation may be caused by the client holding the cash receipts journal open past year-end; i.e., the cash was received and deposited after the balance sheet date, but was recorded as if it were received prior to the balance sheet date. If this were the case, then the year-end cash balance would be overstated.

3. The pattern of dates suggests a possibility of kiting intended to "window dress" the financial statements. The year-end cash balance is overstated by $16,500 on the balance sheet date since the transfer was recorded as a cash receipt prior to year-end, but the disbursement portion of the transfer was not recorded until after year-end.

Assignment 9

1. When possible, the auditor performs two-way testing of inventory test counts. Some test counts are traced from the client's records to the actual inventory items to test for existence, and other counts are traced from the actual inventory items to the client's inventory records to test for completeness. When the client has a large number of inventory items, it may not be possible to trace directly from the client's inventory records to the actual inventory items. In these cases, the client generally uses prenumbered forms to count inventory, and tests counts of inventory items should be recorded for tracing into the client's year-end inventory compilation.

2. During the inventory observation, the auditor should be alert for inventory that appears obsolete or is segregated from other inventory. At year-end, the auditor should examine recent sales activity for inventory items to determine if the carrying value of inventory is above net realizable value.

3. The auditor's primary concern for the shipment received during the inventory observation is that the inventory and related accounts payable are recorded in the same period. The auditor should note the details of the shipment received during the observation. The inventory should be traced to the year-end inventory listing, and the purchase liability traced to the year end listing of accounts payable.

Assignment 10

1. The subsequent event period covers the period from the balance sheet date to the end of audit fieldwork. An example of a subsequent event that would require disclosure is the sale or purchase of a subsidiary after year-end. An example of a subsequent event that would require adjustment is settlement of a lawsuit after year-end if the underlying condition that resulted in the lawsuit existed at year-end.

2. In evaluating whether the financial statements are fairly stated, the auditor must consider whether unadjusted misstatements would affect the decision of a reasonable user of the financial statements. Accordingly, the auditor should consider whether unadjusted misstatements materially affect net income, as well as other bases such as current assets and total assets. If unadjusted misstatements exceed any of the materiality thresholds, it is necessary for the client to record an adjustment if the financial statements are to be considered fairly stated.

End of Solution

Integrated Audit Practice Case

4th Edition